EARLY SETTLERS

OF

ORANGE COUNTY, FLORIDA

Reminiscent—Historic—Biographic

1915

C. E. HOWARD, ORLANDO, FLA.

PUBLISHER

OLD WORTHIES OF ORANGE COUNTY

The late Hon. W. L. Palmer   The late Gen. W. H. Jewell

The late Judge J. D. Beggs

The late Capt. L. C. Horn   The late Judge Cecil Butt

The late Will Wallace Harney,
Orange County's Poet

The late J. P. Hughey   The late Dr. J. N. Butt

Hiram Beasley
Bailiff of Orange County Court from the
earliest days to now

PREFACE

C. E. HOWARD, PUBLISHER

C. E. Howard, native of Pennsylvania, came to Orange County, locating on Lake Jessamine, October, 1883. Sold to Dwight D. Porter, returned to Pennsylvania, came back in 1888 and located permanently in Orlando in 1904. Has followed publishing business and photography. Edited Orlando Star, Orange County Reporter, Reporter-Star, Sentinel, and for the past five years owned and edited the Orange County Citizen. Served as city alderman twelve years, several terms chairman; Secretary Board of Trade for several years and is now chairman District School Trustees.

This volume is dedicated to the tried and true pioneers of Orange County, Florida, many of them gone to a just reward, many still living to enjoy the fruits of their early labors, a host of them not mentioned in this book, those who are, deserving a place in the future archives of the county.

This little work is not intended as more than an introduction to a few of those worthy men who should not be forgotten by the living beneficiaries of their labors nor by posterity, and to whom they will stand debtor.

Some time, some one will need material for a history of the county and for some of it, at least, he may turn to the facts contained in the lives of those mentioned herein.

THE AUTHOR—C. E. Howard.

The Early History of Orange County

THE DAYS OF LONG AGO

By MRS. J. N. WHITNER
SANFORD, FLORIDA

COUNCIL OAK   *J. M. Alden, Artist.*

Whatever of pride and enjoyment we citizens of Orange County may feel in her present day achievements, our sentiment cannot be praiseworthy till we shall have paused and paid our tributes of respect and honor to those of a generation ago, who, by their Christian faith and practice, their sterling characteristics and ability, overcame primitive conditions and made possible within a lifetime the civilization we now enjoy.

There is a duty—a privilege—sacred and binding, which devolves upon the few of us who are left, who have personal recollections of the real pioneers, that can only be performed by ourselves. The day is growing late when if we would be their worthy successors we must arouse and prepare for the use of those who shall write our country's history, reminiscent characteristic sketches of the men and women who laid so well the foundations upon which we have built, of their traditions and ideals, their manners, social life and religious habits, with incidents, anecdotes and facts relative to them.

When the earliest of our county's history shall be evolved from the shadows of the past, and recalled by patient efforts, we shall find it is a part of that story of unsurpassed tragedy and romance, the story of the Seminole wars of nearly a century ago.

For this reason Orange County contains many places of interest, of which now we have only a vague knowledge but when the work is completed of compiling the Seminole war records from the archives at Washington, we hope to obtain information which shall be reliable.

Prominent among these places are the military graveyards of two wars, familiar to many persons and for their care appropriations might be obtained from the United States Government.

Some of the localities are well known, where historic and otherwise prominent events have occurred, where earliest settlements were made (many of these are sacred to us now) and where the dead were laid to rest. Only after the utmost care should data be accepted as authentic, but when satisfactorily established the places should be marked even if at present in very simple manner, and the sentiment which time attaches to such will suggest appropriate and enduring memorials in tablets and stone.

A peculiar pathos lingers around everything connected with the Indians and all over our country are traces of their neighborhood life, and along the St. Johns River, which they called Welaka, are many burial mounds. These mounds, especially, should be preserved from the hands of vandals.

In 1750 the Creek Indians in Alabama separated and many of them emigrated to Florida under a chief name Secoffee and settled in the western part of the peninsula, which they called Alachua. These united with the native tribes of the peninsula and together they absorbed many run-away negro slaves from Georgia. Their descendants became the fierce Seminoles and by the end of the century had over-run the peninsula.

This remnant of the once free, proud, red men, crowded back, and driven before the march of civilization, proved a formidable foe to any who dared encroach upon the sunny strip lying between the ocean and the gulf, the last left to them of all the continent which by Divine right of inheritance and possession had belonged to their people.

The record of the Seminole War of 1836 reported the establishment of Camp Monroe on the south shore of the lake which bears that name, thus opening the route by which the United States army advanced into the interior of the eastern half of the peninsula for the suppression of the Seminole Indians. The post was occupied by two companies of artillery, four companies of dragoons and some Creek Indians.

Can one imagine the indignant horror of the Indians at the sight of these forerunners of the army of their pursuers entering the gateway of their retreat? And they would claim even this!

Leaders arose, stimulated perhaps to a greater degree of daring by slight trace of the blood of white men in the veins of some of them. These poor savages in their extremity arose to the white man's conception of the loftiest heights of valor for the defence of their wigwams and their hunting grounds.

Under the counsel of Oceola, and the leadership of King Philip and Coacoochee, son and grandson of the old chief Secoffee, four hundred braves made a bold and desperate attack upon Camp Monroe on the 6th of February, 1837, a few weeks after its establish-

ment, and but for the greater force of artillery over simple fire arms, the story of the massacre would have been frightful to relate.

With a desperate courage the Indians fought fiercely for three hours. Captain Charles Mellen was killed. Fourteen others were wounded. The Indians' loss was twenty-five. It was said afterwards that the Indians became terrified at the roar of the cannon, with twigs and limbs falling from the trees, and thinking that a thunder storm was raging, sent by the Great Spirit to aid the white men, the poor creatures gave up the attack and fled in terror to the woods.

The military records state that after this attack the name of Camp Monroe was changed to Fort Mellen and became the most important and healthful inland state in Florida; as a base for supplies and distribution for the many forts and military camps which were scattered all over Mosquito Co., the territory of which extended from St. Johns County on the north southward to Monroe, which then extended across the peninsula on the west from Alachua to the Atlantic.

A few of the names of these forts and camps are still perpetuated in our county as Fort Reed, Maitland, Gatlin and Christmas, all having been the scenes of military life.

At Fort Gatlin, now almost within the suburbs of the beautiful county site, Orlando, stands the bleached trunk and bare widespread branches of an immense dead live-oak. It is said that under this oak the red men and the white met to hold a council. At this late day, we can easily believe that the Indians' part in that council was but to listen to the arbitrary sentence which would expel them forever to the cold, bleak plains of the West, away from the fair land that they loved, from its shady hammocks of moss-draped cypress and magnolias, its winding rivers overhung with palms and willows and oaks, red hybiscus and white lilies, its grassy prairies stretching off into rolling forests of lofty pines, dotted here and there with clear blue lakes and the wide stretch of the waters in her inland seas, the happiest hunting ground that Indians ever dwelt upon, where a variety of game roamed in abundance and the rigors of cold were scarcely felt. White men had need of this peerless land, and a council was called to inform the red men of the plans for their departure on the ships to be in waiting for them at Tampa, and our fancy suggests that what the children of the forest heard that day broke the heart of the tree. The Indians are gone. Some went to the West, a few were permitted to remain beyond a line which the white men drew and their descendants still lodge in the swamps of the Everglades.

But the Council Oak stands, her white arms held aloft, a silent protest against the injustice of war, a ghostly presence lamenting her children, a memorial of them, which time, nor storm has expelled in all the years since then. A very beautiful picture has been painted of the Council Oak by a talented member of this association, Mr. Alden, of Orlando. We may find no proofs, but tradition of the story of the oak and the council, but the legend is sweet and we will pass it on.

Before leaving the subjects which will be of interest to our historians, we would particularly emphasize the type of the people whom we have called Orange County's pioneers, as distinct from the adventurous spirits who usually inhabit new countries.

Orange County was populated at two distinct periods, her earliest settlements were a consequence of the Seminole wars, and the second infusion resulted from the unsettled condition of society incident to the Civil war. A large proportion of the soldiers in the Seminole wars were volunteers. When the time came in 1857 that the regular army was withdrawn, some of the volunteer soldiers remained and many of the camps proved the nucleus of a neighborhood, and the fact must be recognized that in the main these made substantial citizens.

From that period till after the Civil War few persons came to the county and few moved away. Some small orange groves were planted and the people produced from the soil mainly what they consumed for food. Large herds of cattle grazed upon the prairies and many

persons (in proportion to the standards of the time) grew wealthy.

1866 ushered in the first glow of a new era. In the great readjustment which was taking place in the states north of us, as if by a simultaneous impulse attention seemed fixed upon Florida. The world heard of her orange groves and her balmy climate. Many families in other southern states, disturbed and unsettled in the plantation life in which they had been reared, turned to new scenes. Accustomed to agricultural pursuits, fruit culture seemed natural and attractive and the result was the removal from those states to this county of a class of persons who had many of them lived on the same soil since their forefathers came to America in the early colonial days. Those from the north sought health, climate or investment, each representing a more refined and cultured type than is usually found among the early settlers of a new territory.

This is a meagre outline of the causes which led to the displacing of the original inhabitants of peninsular Florida, and the rapid filling up of our county, from a period immediately after the Civil War by a population so cosmopolitan that in every audience that assembles almost every state in the Union has its representatives, besides many foreign countries as well. Such conditions might reasonably well have consumed a longer period in adjusting these various elements into a harmonious citizenship, but the spirit and ideals of the majority of them is attested by the public institutions for which they laid the foundations, and upon which their successors have builded, until ours is a civilization of which we may justly feel proud as being equal to, and in some respects superior to what has been achieved in many of the older states.

CAPTAIN B. M. SIMS
CHARTER PRESIDENT ORANGE COUNTY PIONEERS' ASSOCIATION

CAPT. B. M. SIMS

Capt. B. M. Sims, of Ocoee, is a Tennessean, educated at Hiwassee College in that State. Served through the Civil war. Came to Florida in 1865 and found Orange County about 120 miles long by 60 miles wide, with 75 voters; no railroad nearer than Jacksonville, and no postoffice in the County.

He taught school the first year, which was the first school ever taught in Orange County. He built the first frame courthouse in the county—the old courthouse being a log house with a dirt floor.

A few years previous a little colony of wealthy men had settled on South Apopka. The little colony owned over one hundred negroes, and cleared up several hundred acres of rich hammock land for raising Sea Island cotton and sugar cane. Some of the names of the little colony were Hudson, Pigue, Roper, Dr. Stark.

When the war came on, most of the settlers left, the negroes being freed. Capt. Sims rented fifty acres of Dr. Stark's plantation and planted cotton and corn. He raised 2,000 pounds of cotton and one thousand bushels of corn, selling the cotton for $2,000. While he was cultivating the crop he bought a piece of wild hammock land on Lake Apopka with wild orange trees. He cut the wild trees off and put sweet buds in the stumps, and planted

a citrus nursery, which was probably the first mercantile citrus nursery in the United States. He has kept that business up to the present time, furnishing trees for almost all the large old groves in this part of the State, and shipping a great many to California, and has at the present a large, fine nursery.

He is probably the only man living who was selling oranges and trees from his own raising in 1870.

He was the only man owning a ten-acre bearing grove at that time. In 1893, when the "big freeze" came, he owned 60 acres of bearing grove, after having sold 30 acres for thirty thousand dollars.

At that time he owned stock in the Citizens' National Bank of Orlando, and was one of the directors. The freeze caused the bank to break, and the stockholders had their stock doubled on them and lost it all. He was one of the first men to ship vegetables to the North.

He has never held office except County Commissioner. He is the oldest Freemason in the county, and was once District Deputy Grand Master for the State.

He has four children and is able to start them on ten thousand dollars' worth of property apiece. He says he has done his best, has fought a good fight and got licked.

J. WALTER SIMS

J. WALTER SIMS

J. Walter Sims, son of Captain B. M. Sims, is an "Orange County boy," for the very good reason that he was born in Ocoee, where his boyhood and youth were spent amid the orange groves, gardens and native Florida woods.

It was not surprising that, as he studied the map of the United States and noted the vast expanse of the great western domain that he fancied he was a bit too cramped in Ocoee, hence he emigrated, "Westward, Ho!" But he found it wild and woolly and not at all in keeping with good old Orange County, and after giving it a fair trial, he shook the dust of it all off his feet and returned home to live and when done living, to die in Dixie.

DR. EUGENE O. SIMS

Doctor Sims has a right to be called an old settler in that he first saw the light of day at Ocoee, Orange County, Fla., June 11, 1867.

After attending the public schools of that day until twelve years of age, he was sent to the Tullahoma, Tenn., public schools and from there went to Burritt College, Spencer County, Tenn., where he graduated.

Deciding upon dentistry as his profession, he went to the Baltimore College of Dentistry, from which he graduated in 1890.

And now, having an education and a profession, one of the most important as well as most profitable, he had all the world before him to choose where best to locate for the good of the people, as well as for himself.

Of course they needed him right in his own county and near to his own home and the time would come when he would consent to such an arrangement, but first there was the whole world beckoning to him with enticing hand.

The state of Texas held out inducements and he went there to practice dentistry, remaining two years, moved to Brunswick, Georgia, two years, removed to Atlanta for two years and in 1898 went to Honduras for a year and in Cuba two years, finally returning to Ocoee, remained a year, and in 1912 opened an office in Winter Garden. Thus, he holds dental certificates of Florida, Georgia, South Carolina, Maryland, Texas, Cuba.

DR. EUGENE O. SIMS

MURRAY S. KING

MURRAY S. KING

Pennsylvania contributed Murray S. King to Orlando, in 1904.

For several years he followed building and contracting and when the time seemed ripe, took up his profession as architect.

Many of the best buildings in the city and county stand as monuments to his skill and creative genius. Among those that might be mentioned are the Robt. Dhu MacDonald residence in Winter Park, the beautiful Tiedkie mansion on Magnolia avenue, the Astor Hotel, the Grand Theatre, Yowell-Duckworth department building and the Presbyterian church.

Surely a man who adds to the permanent, habitable, business and religious buildings of a city is a citizen worth while, and Florida has long looked forward to the time when men of sufficient foresight would see that her peculiar climate calls for a style and quality of architecture differing in many essentials from that of the frigid and temperate zones, besides the fact that the very environment gives opportunity for many departures into the Spanish Mission, Greek, Roman, Indian and other types, which fit suitably into it with particular suitability.

Mr. King's personal fitness has won for him recently an appointment to the Florida State Board of Architecture, of which he was made president, and he is also a charter member and director in the Florida Association of Architects.

C. A. BOONE

C. A. BOONE

City Assessor and Tax Collector C. A. Boone was one of the earliest citizens of Orlando. There are at this writing four of these first citizens still residents of the city.

He came from North Carolina to Orange County, Florida, in 1870. First he taught school. In 1872, the first public school was established in Orlando; the photograph of the original building is found elsewhere in this book.

Mr. Boone was proprietor of the only hotel in those early days—The Lovell House. He was one of the original merchants, having a general store with W. A. Patrick as partner.

In 1875, Mr. Boone went into the County Clerk's office and held his position until 1881, when he again entered the mercantile field, the hardware business, his old partner, W. A. Patrick associating with him under the firm name of C. A. Boone & Co. This hardware company did a flourishing business, as about this time Orlando and the prosperous section thereabout began to take on its first wonderful growth. In 1893 he sold his hardware business. He was elected Mayor of Orlando in 1883. He also served as City Councilman in the earlier days and was one of the original incorporators of the city in 1875.

From 1893 to 1907, he conducted an extensive dairy and nursery business, the latter occupying much of his personal attention. As an orange grower, he was successful, Boone's Early Orange being one of his productions.

From 1907 to 1914 he was successively elected to the office of City Clerk and Assessor, and under the new Commission city government he holds the position of Assessor and Tax Collector. Mr. Boone has thus lived a busy and honored life among his townspeople from the very beginning of the city.

FRANK H. DAVIS

FRANK H. DAVIS

The native place of Mr. Davis was Manchester, N. H. Born on April 5th, 1854. His father, Dr. E. H. Davis, was a physician and surgeon and practiced medicine in Manchester for more than thirty years; was surgeon in Fifth New Hampshire Regiment in the Civil war. He graduated from the Manchester High School in 1874; being anxious to take up the business activities of life at once, he did not continue his studies as he was privileged to do, but went to Boston, where he secured a position in the counting room of a wholesale house on Summer Street; was there about two years. His attention was first directed to Florida in 1876 through letters from a friend who had settled in this State near Apopka. He came South in October, 1876, and joined this friend. For many years he lived the life of the average first settler; early took up a homestead and set about clearing land for an orange grove.

During those years he occupied bachelors' quarters and roughed it with the rest. At that time Apopka had one mail a week and on Saturday, which was mail day, the one little store in town was the Mecca toward which all steps were tending; no boxes in those days, the mail was distributed directly from the bag. Sanford, or Mellonville, was the base of supplies, and the mail and all goods were brought by team from that point. Later freight and passenger service was furnished via the Wekiva River. Apopka proper was early known as "The Lodge," so called from the old established Masonic Lodge. The Apopka district comprised all the country around Lake Apopka and included Oakland, Ocoee, Winter Garden, and Apopka of the present day. Dr. Mason,

one of the very first settlers of Apopka, was the oracle of wisdom on all matters pertaining to fruit culture; Judge Mills, who figures so prominently in land titles in this section, did the surveying; the Sims Grove on Lake Apopka was the ne plus ultra of orange groves in the county, and Judge Speer, of Oakland, was quite prominent in county affairs.

The life of the early settler was replete with varied and trying experiences. Everything was crude, and there were many deprivations. At times the one store in the settlement was without flour, sugar, butter, and other indispensables of the present day, but there were no fickle appetites, and hog and hominy was not frowned upon if the delectables were lacking. Social gatherings gave zest to life, for the first settler always found time for fun, and then there was the old-fashioned camp meeting, where all repaired once a year to be regaled with explosive exhortations, and incidentally with sweet potato pie and other interesting accessories. The virgin pine forests, untouched by turpentine or mill men, were the special charm of Florida in the old days, through which the roads and trails were well defined and accordingly easily followed. Alas the change! With the passing of the timber came obliteration of old trails, and consequent confusion as to roads and courses and one of the most interesting features of the old Florida has gone from us.

The first railroad was built through Apopka in 1885 and it was during that time that Mr. Davis opened a real estate office and continued in that business, in connection with orange growing, since that time. Latterly he has had trucking interests at Winter Garden, making a specialty of lettuce and cucumbers on sub-irrigated lands from artesian well.

He met with great reverses in 1895 in common with so many others in Florida, and for a time it seemed that he might be compelled to make change of base. He concluded to stick, however, and now is getting a good share of his income from groves that were killed down at the time of the Big Freeze.

Mr. Davis has been prominently identified with public affairs in Apopka. He has served as councilman many times; was active in the organization of the Apopka Board of Trade, and was its first president, holding this office for two terms. He took the oath of office of Mayor in January, 1915.

A. SPEER

A. SPEER AND WIFE

A Speer, the subject of this sketch, was born at Augusta, Ga., October, 1852. His father, Judge J. G. Speer, moved to Florida in 1854, when the son was two years old, when Orange County was almost an unbroken forest, and the highways were little more than cow-paths. Almost his earliest recollection was the moving of the last of the Indians from this state to Indian Territory. His father was living at Ft. Gatlin, when the present county site was located. His parents moved to the present site of Oakland when Mr. Speer was a very small boy, and when there were just a few settlers with miles of forest between them, when the woods were alive with all kinds of game, such as bear, panther, wildcats, deer and turkeys, not leaving out the wolves, which howled within hearing of his home every night and morning. When a deer or turkey was wanted all one had to do was to take his gun (always the rifle) and go get it. After the civil war he went to South Carolina to school.

After returning from there he assisted his father and brother in buying and driving beef cattle to Ft. Myers for the Spanish army during the ten-year war.

In 1874 he took a homestead near Oakland and began clearing land and setting out an orange grove, which he later sold. In 1877 he married Miss Alice Roper, by whom he had a son, W. E. Speer, of Dania, Fla., who is engaged in buying and packing fruits and vegetables. His wife dying in the third year after their marriage, on the fifteenth day of March, 1882, he married Miss M. C. Kincaid, of Murphy, N. C., by whom he has two children, Gertrude K. Speer and James P. Speer. The former has been teaching in the Sanford High School (8th grade) for 8 or 9 years. His son, Jas. P. Speer, is a promising young lawyer, located at Comanche, Okla., and is at present a member of the House of Representatives from Stevens County, Okla.

A. Speer has lived at Oakland almost continuously, built and kept the first store at Oakland, later engaging in farming and fruit growing, has been a justice in the Oakland district for twenty-odd years, and is still holding down the job.

JUDGE J. G. SPEER

Judge J. G. Speer was born in South Carolina, June 23, 1820. His ancestors were sturdy Scotch-Irish. His grandfather, William Speer, came from County Antrim about the beginning of the Revolutionary war, espoused the cause of the colonies, fighting through the war in General Picken's command. Judge J. G. Speer was a staunch defender of the right, though it might be the weaker side, and was independent of popular opinion in taking a stand against what he conceived to be wrong and would never buy success by compromising principle. Coming to Florida at an early date (1854) he became widely known and deservedly esteemed. He took an active part in the organization of the county, which at that time included a large part of Osceola, also a large part of Lake and all of what is now Seminole. He was repeatedly called to places of honor and trust, serving one term in the lower House of the Legislature and two terms in the State Senate. At one time he was a candidate for the U. S. Senate, lacking only one vote of election, causing a deadlock for ten days, at which time he withdrew his name. Two years later he was a candidate before the gubernatorial convention for governor of the state and hung that body several days when he withdrew in favor of Honorable Francis P. Flemming, who was elected.

When duty called him to antagonize a powerful and unscrupulous interest, he did not hesitate. The liquor traffic felt and remembers the blows he gave it in the legislature and before the people. He was in the convention that gave the state its present constitution, and was the author of Article 19 of the constitution, regulating the liquor business. He was living at Ft. Gatlin, near Orlando, when the question of locating the county site came up. This was a three-cornered fight: Ft. Reid, "The Lodge" (so called because here was located the only Masonic Lodge in the county), now Apopka City; and Ft. Gatlin, each place being championed by its settlers. A distant cousin, Dr. Sidney Speer, led the Ft. Reid forces; Isaac Newton led the Lodge crowd, and Judge Speer led the Ft. Gatlin settlers, and Ft. Gatlin won. At once the question of a name came up and was named "Orlando" by Judge Speer for one of Shakespeare's characters.

He was County Judge for several years, until he moved to the section now known as South Apopka. In 1880, he took charge of the Apopka Drainage Company, for the purpose of draining the muck lands on the north of Lake Apopka.

In 1886 he induced the Orange Belt Railroad to come by way of Oakland on its way south, (the road was to have gone some miles south of Oakland), giving the railroad company a half interest in two hundred acres of land on which the town of Oakland is located.

His life and Christian character will leave the most enduring impress on those who knew him best. He died October 31, 1893.

HON. WILLIAM R. O'NEAL

WILLIAM R. O'NEAL

No one man has been so prominently engaged in the up-building of Orange County, in so many varied ways, as William R. O'Neal. Everybody "hands it to him" when it comes to that vital touch that has left an imprint in the business, fraternal, religious, educational and political life of not only the city and county, but the state, as well.

An Ohioan, born of Virginia parentage, he became a law student and made a specialty of insurance in his native state.

An opportunity opened for him to become manager of the Ford estate, which brought him to Orlando, Orange County, in 1886, later engaging in the business of insurance, rentals, collections, real estate and adjustments of estates. The firm was known at that time as Curtis, Fletcher & O'Neal, and later Curtis & O'Neal, and included a profitable book business.

Mr. O'Neal became connected with the educational interests of the county at an early date. In 1887 he became a trustee and secretary and treasurer of Rollins College, and as such he has become vitally connected with the education of many young men and women of the state and elsewhere, not a few of whom are making their mark in the world at this time.

He was for a long time the chairman of the Orlando school trustees and was a positive factor in the promotion of local educational interests.

Politically, Mr. O'Neal is a republican, one of the kind who loyally stuck to his colors when he came South, and for years he has been foremost in the councils and conventions of his party. As such he was the nominee of his party for congress, for governor and for superintendent of public instruction and was in 1898 appointed postmaster of Orlando, retaining the office with great satisfaction to the people until the appointment of his democratic successor in 1915.

For many years he was a city alderman and was president of the city council when, during the hard, constructive period of the city's history, he labored industriously for the best interests of the people.

He is at this time president of the Apopka Bank, a director in the State Bank of Orlando, secretary and treasurer of the Seminole Hotel Company of Winter Park, secretary of the Fair Association and a valued officer in various other business enterprises.

He is prominently identified with several fraternal organizations, notably, the Knights of Pythias, Masons, Commandery, Odd Fellows and Elks.

He is now serving his third term as Supreme Representative of the Knights of Pythias, and is a member of the Board of Control of the Insurance Department.

He is Grand Commander of the Knights Templar of Florida, Deputy Grand Exalted Ruler for the Southern District of Florida, for Benevolent and Protective Order of Elks. Deputy Grand High Priest of Grand Lodge R. A. M.

HON. SAMUEL AUSTIN ROBINSON

SAMUEL A. ROBINSON

Samuel Austin Robinson, of 104 N. Main street, Orlando, Florida, was born in Emmett, near Battle Creek, Michigan, March 12. 1849. and was descended from Puritan and revolutionary sires.

His education was obtained in the public schools of his native county. He engaged in farming on the old homestead, and afterwards taught school one year in Clark County, Ind.

May 25th, 1876, he was married to Miss Mary A. Bird, of Pennfield. Calhoun Co., Mich.

In October, 1876, Mr. and Mrs. Robinson arrived in Orlando, and have since made it their home.

Mr. Robinson engaged in civil engineering and surveying in Florida 30 years, being County Surveyor 16 years. He was then County and State Tax Assessor for five years, and Representative in the Legislature for two terms, from 1910 to 1915. He was once Tax Collector of Orange County, and was Alderman, City Surveyor, Tax Collector, and one of the Trustees of the Orlando Public Schools. He has also been a Notary Public for 35 years. He surveyed the cities of Orlando, Winter Park and Kissimmee, and other towns. He surveyed the Lake Jesup, O. & K. R. Railroad to where the city of Kissimmee now stands, when he saw but four houses south of Bogy Creek on the route.

Those familiar with the early history of Orange County know the agitation of the building of this proposed road had much to do to hasten the building of the S. F. Railroad, which resulted in the building of the cities of Sanford. Orlando, and Kissimmee.

Robinson Avenue. in Orlando. and Robinson Spring. between Orlando and Sanford, were both named for him. He designed and surveyed "Greenwood." belonging to Orlando. and the Lakeland cemetery was copied after it.

Mr. Robinson obtained from Indian mounds and otherwise in Florida. the only large collection of gold and silver ornaments that have been reported in the United States.

Prof. George F. Kunz, the world's great gem expert. examined and described them, and the American Antiquarian, of July, 1887, published his report. They now belong to the Metropolitan Museum of Arts. New York.

He made original research in Florida, and unearthed splendid fossil teeth of the elephant, mastodon, bison, camel. tapir, horse, mylodon, diodon, capybara, and scales of the glyptodon, and many other fossil species.

MAJ. WM. BRIGHAM LYNCH

MAJ. W. B. LYNCH

Born in Orange County, N. C., Jan. 19, 1834, died at his home, Orlando, Orange Co., Fla., July 30, 1911. At the early age of nine he entered the famous Bingham School of North Carolina, thence to the State University, graduating with distinguished honor in the class of 1859, delivering the Latin salutatory oration and was tendered a professorship in the same university, but preferred to accept the chair of Greek in Davidson College, N. C. This position he filled with ability for three years, leaving to organize a company upon the outbreak of the civil war, enlisted in the Confederate service and became captain of his company.

In the army he developed the very highest qualities of the citizen-soldier, true to the highest ideals through all the hardships and toil, and endeared himself, as a commander, to all his men.

At the close of the war, he became co-principal of the Bingham School and held it for sixteen years.

For health considerations he disposed of his interests and moved to Sanford, Orange Co., Fla., in 1882, giving attention to orange growing and teaching. In 1897, he was elected Superintendent of Public Instruction for Orange County and served three consecutive terms of four years each, being elected without opposition, the highest testimonial to his efficiency and faithfulness.

In his long service as superintendent of the county schools he brought to bear a scholarly mind and a polished, agreeable disposition, co-operating gladly and faithfully with officials and teachers and students for the highest interests of education.

DEXTER C. THOMPSON

The subject of this sketch was born in Brockton, Mass., in 1859. Educated in the public schools of that city he early entered business life, coming to Orange County, Fla., in 1881, and located in Sanford, where the terminus of the St. Johns River navigation and the South Florida Railroad enterprise opened up wonderful opportunities for business activity.

Mr. Thompson was possessed of more than ordinary business talent and foresight, added to great capacity and executive ability. Besides, he knew conditions and had a keen insight into men and understood the use of "Time and Tide."

He looked over the field and there was the inevitable opportunity in the rapidly increasing demand for building material, as Sanford itself improved, besides the many towns on the river and the opening up of the new country southward over the line of the South Florida railroad steadily building to Tampa.

All the crude orange box material was at that time sent down from Maine and the increasing orange industry held out promising profit.

For these and a few other reasons the lumber business engaged his attention. From a modest beginning his interests increased so that he finally became president of The Warnell Lumber Company, with mills and factories in several localities, still successfully running, as evidence of his business ability.

Mr. Thompson was a citizen of very genial parts. He, for some years prior to his death lived on Lucerne Circle in the city of Orlando. His health failing, he sought relief in New Mexico, where, on Sept. 12, 1907, he died.

DEXTER C. THOMPSON

LOUIS C. MASSEY

LOUIS C. MASSEY

Among the professional and political men of Orange County and the State of Florida, Senator L. C. Massey stands the peer of any. In the up-building of the county, financially and legally and in the councils of the State, history will record much more of him than can be noted in this brief record.

Mr. Massey is a Pennsylvanian, having been born in Philadelphia, receiving his education in the public schools and the University of Pennsylvania.

After studying law he practiced in his native city until he came to Orlando, Orange County, Florida, in 1885. Soon after, he opened a law office in the county town of Orange, first with Massey, Keating & Willcox, then Massey & Willcox, and finally under the present firm name of Massey & Warlow.

His legal attainments have always been rated among the highest, recognized by Governor Fleming, when he appointed him a commissioner for the revision of the General Florida Statutes, shortly after he had been one of the commissioners of the county, later, when he was appointed by Governor Mitchell a state commissioner on uniformity of legislation, and still later when appointed counsel to the State Railroad Commission.

He was elected City Solicitor of Orlando and State Senator of the 19th Senatorial District, serving with distinction and credit, as a Senator and lawyer always to be depended upon, and bringing distinguished honor upon his district and city.

Since 1911 he has given increased attention to his practice, in addition to the somewhat arduous duties thrust upon him as City Solicitor under the new order of commission government in Orlando.

Fraternally he has been Grand Master of the Masonic Lodge, Grand Commander of Knights Templar, Grand Master of the Royal and Select Master Masons of Florida, and is a member of the Elks.

JOHN T. CHAPMAN

JOHN L. CHAPMAN

A native of Crawfordville, Ga., educated at Mercer University, Macon, Ga. Joined the Confederate army in 1861 and was mustered out in 1864, after honorable service, having been shot three times and a leg broken.

In 1877, Mr. Chapman was a member of the Georgia Legislature. This, in brief, is his history before coming to Orange County, Fla., in 1882, when he taught school at Apopka as introductory to his residence here.

He then went into orange growing and soon became a member of the County Board of Commissioners and then a member of the Florida State Legislature for two years.

All this time he was a busy man, having direct charge of eighteen orange groves in the vicinity of his home in Plymouth.

His family consists of Mrs. Chapman, who was Miss Meadows, of Herd County, Ga., and eight children: E. G. Chapman, William A. Chapman, Miss Mattie P. Chapman, Mrs. Rachel E. Overstreet, Dr. John C. Chapman, Mrs. Annie B. Wiggs, Thomas A. Chapman, Mrs. E. Judson Rawls.

Full of years and with the ripe results of a busy and useful lifetime to his credit, Mr. Chapman now enjoys the peace and tranquility of a happy Florida home life in the favored section of Orange County known as Plymouth, respected and loved by all his neighbors and honored by the citizens of the county.

HON. GEORGE W. CRAWFORD

Mr. Crawford is a native of Tennessee, and prior to moving to Florida was a clerk in the store of Harry Loveless, at Como, Tenn. He came to Conway, Orange County, Fla., in 1873, and immediately took up the favorite occupation of orange growing and farming, including stock-raising, and has long been known successful in this honorable occupation.

His soldier life was served with honor in the Confederate Army, 5th Tennessee Infantry, and out of a roll of thirteen hundred he was one of thirty who were left to surrender under Gen. Joseph E. Johnson at Saulsbury, N. C.

But it is as a citizen-farmer that he is best known in Orange County.

He was the very first Florida farmer the writer met upon entering the State and his quiet, practical presentation of farming and fruit-growing possibilities is vividly remembered as a prophecy of what has come to pass.

His public life in Florida was serving as Justice of the Peace for two years and was elected a member of the Florida Legislature in 1901, holding this distinguished position through 4 successive terms to 1907.

Among the important bills passed and in which he was proud to serve his people was that empowering the County Commissioners to plant shade trees on the public highways.

Respected and loved for his sterling qualities, this old gentleman is a type of the old settler who has made good for himself, and particularly for his neighbors.

HON. G. W. CRAWFORD

DR. WASHINGTON KILMER

W. KILMER, M. D.

Doctor Kilmer has been a resident of Florida since 1872, and his way of coming here is rather unique compared with this day of fine parlor cars and many automobiles.

Born in Schohant, N. Y., in 1838, he is as finely a preserved man as there is in the State, and yet he walked from Ironton, Ohio, in 1872, a trip of 1,453 miles, on account of a physical breakdown.

He undertook this interesting trip as a correspondent for the Cincinnati Commercial, Murat Halstead, editor, and traveled over the mountains of West Virginia, coming out at Wakalla, S. C., thence through Georgia and Florida, perfectly restored in physical vigor. After a short time spent North, he returned in March, 1873, and located at Altamonte, to which beautiful spot in Orange County he gave the name it is now known by.

Here he became active in educational matters, serving on the County School Board for eight years, helping to lay the school system of the county and assisted in inaugurating the first teachers' institute. There was a grange in the county in 1875 and being interested in agriculture and horticulture he was a lecturer for this grange, as well as of the Fruit Growers' Association of that time.

In 1887 yellow fever broke out in Tampa, and there was a hurried call for physicians. Dr. Kilmer was the only one who responded and for five weeks faithfully worked in that stricken city and when he was about to return he was taken down and barely escaped death.

Upon his return to Orlando the people of this city presented him with a gold watch and chain, containing this inscription: "Presented to Dr. Washington Kilmer by the citizens of Orlando in appreciation of his services in the yellow fever epidemic at Tampa, Fla., Nov. 25, 1887."

For fifteen years the doctor was surgeon for the Seaboard Air Line Railroad, and has practiced in Orlando for thirty years. He has seen the building of three successive court houses and practically every house in the city for many years past.

The doctor has two daughters, his wife dying December, 1906.

L. F. TILDEN AND WIFE

In the early days of 1877, Mr. L. F. Tilden left Grundy County, Ill., and journeyed to Apopka, Orange County, Florida, where he purchased 160 acres of land, built a house and lived for two years. The great possibilities of South Lake Apopka impressed him even in those early days and later buying 561 acres on the lake, having a frontage of a mile and a half, he removed to this part of the lake and entered into orange growing, planting and cultivating groves.

As the years passed, the wisdom of his se-lection became more and more apparent, and now this entire region "blossoms as the rose" and is "flowing with milk and honey." The roses are literal, and the milk and honey con-sist of vast orange groves and truck gardens with as delightful a place to live as the world affords.

Mr. Tilden is now eighty years of age and his wife is seventy-four. For fifty-five years they worked together. Four children lived within a half mile and twenty-four grandchil-dren live to call these fine old people blessed.

JUDGE T. PICTON WARLOW

JUDGE T. PICTON WARLOW

The legal and judicial conditions obtaining in Orange County must be typed by the character of the men of that profession.

Only a few of the earlier lawyers of the county remain to give poise to the bar and the courts of today. Among them must be considered Judge T. Picton Warlow, a man with judicial temperament, caution, fair-minded, but withal positive, a man well suited to the honorable position of Judge of the criminal court of the county.

T. Picton Warlow is of English parentage, though born in India.

He was educated in France and Switzerland, and in 1884 arrived in Orlando, Florida. He decided upon the profession of law and was admitted to the bar in 1888, going into the office of Massey & Willcox. In '94 he became a partner in the firm of Massey &

Warlow, which became the prominent law firm in this part of the State.

In 1907 he was appointed county solicitor, and in 1911, upon recommendation of the County Democratic Executive Committee, he was appointed judge of the County Criminal Court, to which he was in 1912 elected.

With Senator Massey, he assisted in the organization of the State Bank of Orlando and is its vice-president. His business relations and capabilities brought him into prominence in the Orlando Board of Trade, upon which he served as president and as a member of the Executive Committee.

His fraternal association has been with the Masons and Elks, of which he is a very prominent member, having been deputy grand master for the 13th district of Florida, F. and A. M., grand high priest of the Royal Arch Masons, and exalted ruler of the Orlando B. P. O. E.

JOHN NEILL SEARCY

JOHN NEILL SEARCY

The paternal ancestor of the subject of this article emigrated from Italy to England from there to North Carolina. His maternal ancestors came from England and Ireland before the Revolution. His maternal great-grandfather, Col. Matthew Martin, moved from South Carolina to Bedford County, Middle Tennessee, in the early settlement of that county. Both of his grandfathers fought under General Jackson in the war of 1812. His grandfather, Robert Searcy, was clerk of the Federal Court in Nashville, Tenn., and the second Grand Master of Masons. His father, Dr. James Searcy, was born in Nashville, Dec. 8th, 1812. He married Miss Sarah Clay Neill, daughter of Col. Jno. L. Neill. They raised seven children to manhood and womanhood. John was born near the village of Fairfield, Bedford County, March 15th, 1842. His father moved with his family to Panola County, Miss., in the fall of 1855. He was living there when the Civil war began. His oldest brother and he, in May, 1861, joined the Pettus Artillery, commanded by Capt. Alfred B. Hudson, who was killed at the battle of Shiloh. They changed the name of the company to "The Hudson Battery." James L. Hoole then took command of the company.

but owing to ill health commanded it but for a short time. Lieutenant Robert Sweeney then took command until the siege of Vicksburg, where he was killed. The command then fell to Captain Edwin S. Walton. He was severely wounded, but recovered and retained command until they were paroled at Gainesville, Ala., May, 1865. Those who were in the siege at Vicksburg can fully appreciate and sympathize with the hunger and suffering of the Belgians, as they could easily eat their three days' rations at one meal without appeasing hunger. They found mule meat very good and quite "filling." After the fall of Vicksburg they were under General Forest until the surrender and were paroled May 12th, 1865, at Gainsville, Ala. He has his parole framed and hung up over the mantle—a priceless souvenir. After the war his father moved back to Bedford County, he remaining in Bedford County until March 17th, 1873, when he started to Florida, came up the St. Johns River on the steamer Starlight, landed at Melonville on the 23rd, went out to Fort Reid after dark. Next morning he looked out at the palmetto flats and thought to himself, have I left good old Tennessee to starve in this desert? He started to Maitland, met a good old Georgia Cracker who persuaded him to stop with him. He homesteaded land near the town of Longwood. He had good sport with the Cracker, hunting deer where Longwood now stands. When E. W. Henck built the railroad from Sanford to Orlando, he was with the surveying party. On the second day of February, 1885, he married Miss Eva L. Muzzy. Three boys were born to them, one of whom is now living—Charles Blanchard. His wife was born in Gardner, Maine, but was raised in Middle Tennessee. She is the daughter of Eden Muzzy, whose wife was Miss Sarah A. Wallerfield, of Gardner, Maine.

JUDGE WILLIAM MARTIN

JUDGE WILLIAM MARTIN

William Martin is a native of North Carolina and came to Orange County in 1884, locating at Apopka, then the best known place in the county, and where a number of citizens of Orlando first located.

After practicing law until 1887, he moved to the county seat, Orlando, and went into the office of Abrams & Bryan, Judge Bryan being his close friend.

In 1890 he was elected Justice of the Peace and later was elected County Judge, which office he has held for sixteen years.

Judge Martin is a fraternal man of a number of organizations, known and liked by all his associates.

When one visits the courthouse he naturally gravitates to the County Judge's offices, the second door to the right of the entrance, and he generally sees seated at his desk a quiet unassuming gentleman who will greet one and all pleasantly and yet with a certain reserve, which is the outer door left ajar to the good and generous heart of a man who is not given to exclamation points, but who holds his friends closely and attends to his duties with extraordinary fidelity.

It is because of these traits of character that Judge William Martin has held the office he fills for so long a period as sixteen years and probably will continue to hold as long as he wants it or can be prevailed upon to keep it.

HON. A. B. NEWTON

Mr. Newton is a Mississippian, having been born in Itawamba County, that state, in 1864.

He received his education in the common schools and academies of that county.

He was first married to Miss Minnie Odella Harrison, at Tilden, in 1887. In 1892 he came to Orange County, Fla., locating in Winter Garden. His wife died in 1893, and in 1898 he married Miss Alice Bennett Carothers, of Shannon, Miss.

Mr. Newton is a man whom his fellow citizens regard so highly, in whom they have so much confidence that they insist he must serve them.

Since his twenty-fifth year, Mr. Newton has held a number of public offices. At that early age, he was elected Superintendent of Public Instruction in his home county. In 1904 he was a presidential elector on the Parker and Davis ticket.

In 1909 he served as a member of the Florida Legislature and was instrumental in fashioning several important measures.

In 1915 he was again elected to the Legislature, where his influence was always on the right side of public questions and his influence was invariably used for the general good of the people. He is regarded as a man of poise and courage in his section, a busy business man, having held the position of agent for the Coast Line and the Tampa & Gulf railroads, engaged in orange buying and packing, was editor of the "Richochet," and later owner and editor of "The Orange County Citizen," which he sold to C. E. Howard. Also carried on a large mercantile business.

HON. A. B. NEWTON

SHERIFF C. M. HAND

SHERIFF C. M. HAND

C. M. Hand is now the sheriff of Seminole County, Fla., but before Seminole was born of Orange County, he was an old citizen, having landed in Melonville in 1879, locating at Fort Ried.

His father, Henry Hand, opened a blacksmith's and wagon shop at this place, one of the first in the county and later took up a homestead on the Wekiwa River, near Longwood, where he made an orange grove, which the "great freeze" destroyed, necessitating the removal of the family to Sanford.

Here C. M. Hand engaged in the livery business and general contracting for several years, was deputy sheriff of Orange County, elected chief of police of the city, and also mayor.

Upon the division, which created Seminole County out of Orange, he was appointed by the Governor, Sheriff of Seminole and in the first election was elected Sheriff, which, at the time of this writng, he holds.

Sheriff Hand was one of the enthusiastic Sanford men who believed in home rule for his city and thought a division should be made of what is now Seminole County from Orange. He is a hustler and it is said of him that he makes a good officer and is very satisfactory to his constituents.

He is a great lover of sport, and if there is anything doing in ball games he is sure to be somewhere within sight of the diamond. The boys think Charlie Hand is a right hand man because of his convival and jovial temperament, and while the law-breaker may fear arrest at his hands, he well knows that here is a sheriff who can do his duty and remain humane in his treatment of a prisoner.

J. W. MATCHETT

Here is a man who wrestled with Nature and made her divulge the secret of giving up the best of her fruits. He marked out a line around Lake Conway, dammed it up and told the lake to come no farther, dug a deep well for flowing water, drained his muck land to serve for drainage and irrigation.

Mr. Matchett is a born Floridian, his birthplace being Eureka, Marion County, in 1863. He came to Pine Castle, Orange County, a boy, in 1874 and attended the public school, such as it was, and on arriving at manhood clerked in the store of J. M. Blitz for a year. Feeling the need of a business education, he attended Moore's Business College in Atlanta, Ga., a year, and returned to Pine Castle and engaged with C. R. Tyner as clerk and bookkeeper. Later, he filled the same position in C. R. Tyner's general store at Plant City, having general charge of the business.

Returning to Pine Castle he taught school at Oak Ridge, of which Taft is now a part. Within two years he was again engaged in merchandising, superintending the general store of Albert Thompson, being appointed postmaster of Pine Castle at this time, holding the office for eight years. Six years of school teaching followed and then he engaged in citrus fruit culture and vegetable growing, which has been successful.

He was elected justice of the peace three times, serving twelve years. In 1895 was elected Superintendent of Pine Castle Sunday School and has held this place for twenty years, being also Deacon and Clerk of the Baptist Church.

J. W. MATCHETT

L. J. DOLLINS
SECRETARY ORANGE COUNTY PIONEERS' ASSOCIATION

L. J. DOLLINS

The subject of this sketch was born on a farm in Franklin (now Moore) County, Tennessee, on February 24th, 1851. He moved with his father and family to Coffey County about 1857-8. Here the lad with his older brother, Hugh, and sister, Mary, attended such schools as the time and country afforded, the family removing to Saline County, Illinois, in 1863.

Having abandoned everything in their Tennessee home in troublous times, they arrived in their new home at the beginning of winter with only ten dollars, and he and his brother Hugh engaged in rail splitting, while the father, being a skilled farmer, got employment assisting the neighboring farmers in farm work. A farm was in the meantime purchased, and business of home-making started. The children attended the country schools. As the lad advanced he entered the Harrisburg High School, where he graduated in 1872-3. By this time he had begun teaching school. In 1873-4, he went to Lebanon, Ohio, where he took a Normal course, after which he returned to his home school and taught his fourth term in the five years. His health failing in December, 1875, he came to Orange County, Fla., arriving at Lightwood Camp, kept by A. C. Miller, on the 29th day of January, 1876. Was married in June following to Miss Alice Strickland of his home town in Illinois, and settled on a homestead on the 14th of August, 1876. Here he resided five years, dividing the time between school-teaching and farming. Was appointed Deputy Clerk of the county under Mr. J. P. Hughey in September, 1881, and served one and one-half years. His wife died in May, 1882, leaving him with one child four years old. He studied law and was admitted to the Bar in 1885.

In 1883 he was married to Miss Kellie Rushing, of Arkansas, with whom he lived until December, 1893, when she died, leaving the husband with five children, four of her own and one by former marriage. These children are: Mrs. W. S. Jones, of Orlando; Mr. Hugh D. Dollins, of Washington, D. C.; Thomas A. Dollins, of Roanoke, Va., Mrs. John W. Jones, of this city, and Lieutenant Carl W. Dollins, of Jacksonville, Florida. Mr. Dollins after remaining single for nearly seven years, was married to Miss Alice J. Roberts, a former school-mate, of Hillsboro, Tenn., with whom he is living. For several years, he retired to his farming interests, but in 1902 he opened an office for the practice of law, and did a small real estate business. He has straightened out many kinks in titles and estates, and rendered many knotty problems, that hindered progress, easy of solution. He built the Dollins block in 1887. He built for himself and others several fine homes, and now resides at his elegant home place at 728 West Central Avenue.

WILLIAM P. BLAKELY

WILLIAM P. BLAKELY

Mr. Blakely is a native of Tennessee, the city of Nashville, and decided to go to Florida when he finished his education in the High School of Columbia and Carson and Newman College, Jefferson City, Tenn.

Casting about for a suitable location, he selected Orange County, upon the recommendation of W. G. White, the merchant prince of Orlando at that time (1881). Upon locating at Ocoee he was employed by Captain B. M. Sims, and with him, as the foremost citrus grower of the county, learned all the secrets of this fascinating business, and there was much to learn, as nearly all the old groves were clumps of trees planted about the houses of the early settlers or budded on sour wild trees found in the woods. The few men, like Captain Sims, who followed orange growing for profit, had it all to learn—the soil, its needs, fertilization, the best trees to select, the nature of the tree, the enemies and the friends of the fruit.

After two years of this employment he, in 1883, accepted the position of school teacher, as that part of the county began to grow, and held this position during twelve terms. In the meanwhile he devoted attention to bringing up an orange grove and had a fine prospect of bearing groves when the destructive cold of 1905 wiped them out. While working to resuscitate his trees, he conducted the mercantile business bought of John Hughey, and served as postmaster from 1907 till 1915. He held one county office, that of Justice of the Peace during 1885-88.

MRS. C. V. CALDWELL

Mrs. Caldwell came to Orlando, Florida, from Danville, Pa., in 1887, and securing the Summerlin Hotel on Lake Eala, converted it into a select tourist house and all the years since she has made of it a resort to which patrons delight to come.

In the old days this hotel was the headquarters of many politically inclined and if walls had as many tongues as they are said to have ears, the dining room of this old place could tell many a story.

As it is, a mere step onto its shaded porches brings into fond remembrance many of the old-time faces—among them Major Marks, Doctor Foster Chapman, Hardy Garrett, Edbert Allen, Willis L. Palmer, Walter Smith, Seth Woodruff, Major Bradshaw, Dr. Kilmer, Dr. Porter, Edward Hudnal, Jerome Palmer, and many others, some of them now in the world beyond, others still active in the affairs of Orange County and elsewhere.

The newer places of resort spring up all about us, but Mrs. Caldwell's "Summerlin House," so long as it stands, will linger fondly in the minds of the older settlers of Orange County.

J. B. CLOUSER

J. B. CLOUSER

J. B. Clouser was born in Perry County, Pennsylvania, Oct. 15th, 1838, was raised on a farm, chose the trade of a carpenter, at which he worked until he entered the army of the North in the civil war. Was a member of the 149th P. V. Co. D. ("Buck Tails"); was discharged at the end of the war and resumed his trade, and was married in Nov., 1865. He bought and cleared up a home in Center Township, Perry County, Pa., where he lived till November, 1881, when he, with his wife and two children, removed to Orange County, Fla., settled at Longwood, which was a town staked off in the woods, the streets not yet being cut out; built the Longwood Hotel for E. W. Henck, then took charge of the novelty works of P. A. Demans, Longwood, as foreman. At this time it was the only planing mill and novelty works south of Jacksonville. At that time, instead of hearing the whirr and clatter of machinery, one heard the crack and yell of the Florida cow boys, and the public roads were merely crooked, surface roads, or more properly, trails with no bridges. Th

South Florida Railroad was then under construction, having been completed as far as Orlando. The rolling stock consisted of one coach, one flat-car and a diminutive little engine called "The Seminole." But it was a surprise to see the thing speeding along through the wilderness of Orange County. There was no telegraph connection with the outside world till the year after.

Orange culture was then in its infancy. No school houses. Schools were held in private houses, or rather, shanties. Now, there is a good school house and public library, several churches, hotel, good residences with modern improvements, good roads, hard surfaced—some with clay, some brick.

The freeze of 1895-6 was a hard experience, but pluck and perseverance bridged over the hard places and proved a "blessing in disguise." When he arrived in Longwood in 1881, the only hotel accommodations were a bale of hay and an old blanket in the upper story of a box board shanty.

After four years in the employ of P. A. Demans, he, his son, C. A. Clouser, and F. J. Niemeyer, his son-in-law, embarked in the merchantile business, till 1911, when his wife died, when he retired from business. His son, C. A. Clouser, had withdrawn from the firm of J. B. Clouser & Co. previous to this and moved to New Smyrna, Fla., where is in the automobile business, and F. J. Niemeyer carried on the business of their store under the firm name of F. J. Niemeyer.

It is gratifying to note the many changes for the better in the thirty-five years of residence here in Florida.

CHARLES H. HOFFNER

THE OLD WAY

Mr. Hoffner was born in Muscatine, Iowa, in 1856, and lived in Havana, Ill., until 1878. At that time he went to Litchfield, Minn., where he married Miss Edna I. Angier in 1886.

Florida held out a beckoning hand, and in 1889 he moved to Orlando, where he lived for three years and then settled on the Randolph Peninsula of Lake Conway, where he has resided since. He has developed that section from a lonesome settler's home to a village of homes and has assisted in bringing it into close connection with surrounding places by means of newly constructed roads.

Mrs. Hoffner was born in Clearwater, Minn., in 1865, moved to Litchfield, and graduated in the schools of that place in 1882. They have had five children, all living except Lawrence, who died in infancy.

Harry A. graduated from the Orlando High School in 1911, held a responsible position in Orlando and is at this writing filling a position of trust in Jacksonville.

THE NEW WAY

BENJAMIN LUTHER GRIFFIN

B. L. GRIFFIN

MRS. B. L. GRIFFIN

B. L. Griffin was born in Telfair County, Ga., Nov. 20, 1858. His father was Yancey R. Griffin and his mother Rebekah Wilcox, daughter of Gen. Mark Wilcox, for whom Wilcox County was named. Gen Jno. Coffee, his grandfather, also had a Georgia county named for him.

Mr. Griffin came to Orange County, Fla., December, 1879. As there was no railroad, he came by boat to Sanford, from which point on the St. Johns all supplies were hauled over such roads as the country afforded. Ox or horse carts were the usual means of conveyance—two-wheel carts, the man riding the mule and the family in the cart. The fortunate owner of a buckboard was quite up-to-date.

The men in the county were nearly all bachelors and there were few ladies. Mr. Griffin married Miss Henrietta E. Griffin in 1883. She was born in Guinnett County, Ga., in 1864, her father, Dr. Able Griffin, coming to Orange County in 1880. Her brother built the first saw and grist mill in this section, located at the Iron Bridge on the Orlando-Oakland road.

Mr. Griffin contracted to cut ties for what is now the A. C. L. Railroad, the first being a narrow gauge road, and often when the train was overloaded, he put his sturdy shoulder to the car and helped it move along the high places. His wife, before marriage, at the age of seventeen, lived with her brother at Longwood, and during her stay of eight months made the acquaintance of one young lady. Girls did not run about much in those days. This brother, Jno. W. Griffin, bought a large grove of Mr. Jas. Fudge, near Longwood, and also 6,000 acres of land north of Kissimmee, at that time within Orange County.

The family has lived in Orange County all these years and is composed of the father, mother, A. Lee, a son 25 years old, and E. Luther, the younger son, 21 years of age.

S. J. T. SEEGAR

S. J. T. SEEGAR AND WIFE

Mr. Seegar is a northeast Georgian and came to Orange County, Florida, in the year 1884. He engaged in saw-milling, which he successfully followed for four years. Since that time he followed fruit and vegetable growing with great success, now the owner of two orange groves and cultivates thirty acres in vegetables. Mr. Seegar has a family of six children.

Mr. Seegar chose well when he selected the beautiful and thrifty Ocoee section for his home. It is one of the best of farming and fruit-growing localities in Orange County and is a wonderfully thrifty community and during the orange season its busy packing houses and railroads make it one of the busy places on the map.

EDWARD MALTEN STRONG

Virginia and Georgia have been the greatest contributors to Orange County's earlier growth, and these early settlers brought within themselves very strong characteristics in knowledge, determination and stick-to-it-iveness necessary to eventual success as pioneer builders in a new county. Without men of this nature, Orange County would have remained a wilderness and with such men it has progressed by virtue of pure strength of manhood.

Some of these men, naturally, must have been developers of the soil, masters of the forest, growers of the fruits, and others, timber workers and house builders, all of them necessary to a wholesome and uniform growth of the county.

The subject of this article came to Orange County, Florida, from Bedford County, Va., Feb. 3, 1881, landing at Astor, on the St. Johns River. His original intention was to take up a homestead, but owing to some trouble in land matters he went into other lines.

Contracting and carpentry engaged his attention, as well as the culture of oranges.

In 1885 he was marshal of the town of Apopka. On Feb. 22, 1893, he married Miss Witt, who is also a native Virginian.

Mr. Strong's father and brother served in the Confederate army, from which they were honorably discharged.

EDWARD M. STRONG

HENRY NEHRLING

HENRY NEHRLING

Henry Nehrling was born May 9, 1853, at Howard's Grove, Sheboggan County, Wis. His parents were Carl Nehrling and Elizabeth Ruge Nehrling, both from Efurt, Thuringia, Germany.

His parents and grandparents came over to this country in 1852, settling in the primeval forest of white pine and hardwood trees of Town Hermann, Sheboggan County, Wis.

"In this wild, but beautiful region," says a writer in "Wisconsin Men of Progress," "Henry Nehrling received his first and lasting impressions. He was taught to read and write by his mother and grandfather, and was then sent to the Lutheran Parochial School near Howard's Grove. He had to walk over three miles to this school through the forest, which was very beautiful and scarcely touched by the settler's axe."

Such an experience could not fail to make a deep impression upon a boy alive to the beauties of nature, and Henry Nehrling came to manhood with a passionate love for the beauties of the forest and field.

In 1869 he entered the Teacher's Seminary in Addison, DuPage County, Ill., and graduated in June, 1873. He became teacher in a Lutheran school in Harlem, a suburb of Chicago, and obtained a similar position in the city of Chicago in 1876. His favorite books were works on travel, particularly on travel

of naturalists in the tropics. Ornithology and botany were his favorite studies. He did not only study books on the subject, but went out on the prairie and in the forest.

Always having been a lover of the South, he left Chicago in February, 1879 and made Houston, Texas, and later, Lee County, Texas, his home—mainly to study the bird and plant life. He took a position in a private school, as a means of livelihood, and devoted all his leisure hours to the study of his favorite subjects.

In 1883 he bought a piece of land at Gotha, Fla. In 1887, General Conrad Krez, collector of customs for the fort of Milwaukee, appointed Henry Nehrling as his deputy and this position he held also under General Krez's successor. In 1890 he was appointed custodian of the public museum, which position he held for about thirteen years.

The life work of Mr. Nehrling is his great book "Native Birds of Song and Beauty," 2 vols., also in German under the title "Die Nordamerkamische Vogelwelt." These works appeared between 1889 and 1896. It cost him 18 years of study and observation, and scarcely ever has a work been received with such enthusiasm by the critics and nature lovers. The hundreds of reviews that appeared in this country and abroad were all extremely favorable. We take pleasure in quoting only one written by that great naturalist—Dr. Elliot Cones, for "The Auk" (Vol. XIV, 1897, p. 336):

"No more attractive and presentable volumes on our birds are now before the public; and we trust that this labor of love, as it certainly has been on Mr. Nehrling's part, may meet with the full measure of recognition it so well deserves.."

The people of Orange County can well be proud of having the most beautiful garden within their boundary lines—"the finest garden west of Palm Beach, and the richest in plants in all the state," as one expert has proclaimed. I refer to Dr. Henry Nehrling's magnificent collection of plants at Gotha, about ten miles west of Orlando. It is a pity that the road from the village of Gotha to the Palm Cottage grounds is in such a frightful condition. Being a thorough scholar, Mr. Nehrling has, of course, always the scientific side of gardening in view. But in spite of this his grounds, covering about ten acres of land, are rich in beautiful landscape effects. There are cozy nooks and corners everywhere and tangled masses of climbing plants reaching from one tree to the other. Native trees, particularly magnolias, predominate. Mr. Nehrling is of the opinion that our native evergreen trees and shrubs should form the foundation of all our plantings. The flora of Japan and China follow next. We have seen how glorious evergreen shrubs and trees which we never had seen before—Cleyeras, Camellias, Viburnums, Raphilolepis and many others. And how grand are the many beautiful specimens of palms!

The Amaryllis are the glory of the garden in March and April—all Mr. Nehrling's own hybrids, the finest in existence. "Nehrling's Hybrid Amaryllis," so often mentioned in Reasoner Bros. and Dreer's catalogues, have a world-wide fame. And from May to November the indescribably gorgeous color effects of more than 150,000 Caladiums are a sight to see. This is the largest collection of fancy Caladiums consisting at present of about 2,000 distinct varieties. A large number of new varieties originated under Mr. Nehrling's hands, and the most gorgeous he named after his lady friends.

One variety with satiny plum-colored center and golden zone was named Mrs. Marian A. McAdow; another one, velvety glowing crimson, received the name Mrs. Jessie M. Thayer; a variety with a transparent rosy red center, bears the name of Mrs. Frances Laughlin. A bright rosy red kind was called Mrs. W. L. Palmer; a variety with beautiful lavender colored leaves will be known under the name of Mrs. H. L. Beeman and many others too numerous to mention. Though all the Caladiums grown here are extremely beautiful, these new kinds show a very decided improvement.

Mr. Nehrling is a very busy man, having besides his daily work in the garden, a large amount of literary work to perform. But he it always delighted to meet cultured people in his grounds and he is a most charming entertainer. Northern people, seeing these grounds for the first time, cannot help but exclaim: "Oh, what an earthly paradise! How is it possible that such a luxuriant plant life can maintain itself on such a poor sand-hill?"

The demonstration that this can be done is before our eyes. Mr. Nehrling has set an example of what can be done on high pine land with knowledge, patience, love and enthusiasm and adaptatation to circumstances. Orlando, Winter Park, Maitland are fast becoming winter resorts. They are bound to become still more so in the future. One of the best colleges in the South, Rollins College, is located in this region. Rich Northern people, cultured and refined, are building costly winter homes everywhere. They naturally look around to find out what they can do to adorn their place properly. They feel instinctively that Northern trees and shrubs cannot and ought not to find a place in their grounds. What really will do well—the most beautiful native and exotic plants—can be easily seen in this garden, and Mr. Nehrling is always willing and very obliging to give his advice free to everybody who asks for it. Being a philanthropist in the best sense of the word he always finds pleasure in helping people along.

JAMES BAILEY MAGRUDER

J. B. MAGRUDER

"Bailey" Magruder, as he is familiarly known, has had a remarkable Florida experience. He is a constructor and had he the advantages of a Vanderbilt in wealth, he would build a city.

Very few men amid discouragements and hard knocks could show so much as a result of their labor as Mr. Magruder, who is possessed of faith, foresight, grit and get-there far above the average man.

In 1872 he was brought by his father, Major C. B. Magruder, to Rock Ledge, Indian River, from Georgia. His trading proclivities developed at an early age, for at fifteen he was master of a boat and started the first trading boat on the Indian River, when the settlers of all that region depended upon the periodical visits of these stores on boats for their groceries and general goods. Even the Seminole Indians eagerly looked for Magruder's boat and freely traded with him for such articles as captured their fancy.

In 1878 he decided to move to Orange County and first located at Lake Howell, and engaged in orange growing, in time having as many as seventeen groves in cultivation. He established a livery business in Sanford, also buying and selling horses, mules and wagons. While trading thus extensively he, like many others, touched bottom when the great freeze swept everything away, losing 95 per cent of all he owned.

In 1900 he decided to remove to Orlando, where he went into the livery and sales business. Gradually he bought up various properties until he became possessed of splendid orange groves, farms and city property.

His first building venture was "The Arcade," now occupied by the United States postoffice, Southern Express Company, Branche's Book Store, Sentinel Printing office and a dozen other lines, besides a large rooming house.

His next building venture was "The Lucerne Theatre," a long-needed improvement and the best opera house Orlando has ever had. Then he built a new brick livery stable, following that with "Oak Lodge," a large rooming house in the eastern part of the city, and completed his extensive constructive operations to this date by erecting the large four-story Empire Hotel.

W. J. HILL

W. J. HILL

W. J. Hill is the oldest business man in the hardware line in Florida, and claims to have lived longer in Sanford that anyone else.

"Funny how I came to Florida in the first place," said he. "I was born in London, England, March 15th, 1842. I came to New York in July, '72. I worked as an interpreter in the election race of Grant and Greeley, as most of the people did not understand the Cockney language. Worked at this until the election was over. It was cold and uncomfortable. One day I met an Englishman I knew. 'Tell me,' said I, 'Where do all of the blooming swells go when it gets like this?' 'To Florida, my chap,' said he, and to Florida this swell immediately went.

"Our steamer stopped at Savannah, and I bought a map, and started to walk to Florida, as it looked a short distance on the map. I walked until I came to about a half dozen houses, and I asked a lady if that was Florida, and she laughed, and asked me where I came from, and said, 'No, young man, this is Jessup, Georgia.' I then made my way from there by train and boat until I got to Jacksonville. At that time it was a mud-hole. I went south with two Georgia men, who were going to Fort Meade. They had hired a man and boat to take them south, and asked me to go with them, which I did. We landed at the place now called Sanford; then, the smallest place

in the world, and I had come from the largest place.

"I looked about. Not even a policeman around, and you may be sure there was nobody else. Everything was bathed in warm sunshine. It was just the place I wanted. I saw tropical trees loaded with fruit. The river, we knew, swarmed with fish. We caught sight of a covey of quail. I made a quick decision. 'Captain,' I said, 'I will stop here.' So we were left there with nothing but guns and ammunition.

"The first night we slept on the ground. At least they did. I was too scared of snakes. I got up and took a walk, still scared of snakes. I lay down, but you should have seen me get up. I thought I was bitten by a snake, and I hallowed, and asked them to do something for me, as I should soon die. So they tried to find the place where I was bitten, and pulled out a sand spur. I asked them what animal it was that bit me, or was it one of those stingarees, that I had heard the boatmen talking about. Should I die? And they said that I would have to be very careful, and put pine gum on it, which I did. When night came, I couldn't get my pants off. They stuck to the gum. They had to cut a piece out to get them off. I sent that sand spur to my sister in England to show her what I had been through.

"The next day the Georgia men started to Fort Meade. I went with them for about three miles. I asked an old gentleman (Aleck Vaughn's father, sitting in an orange grove with no fence around it, 'What is the name of this place?' He told us that it was Fort Ried. I said, 'Let us go to the Fort and see the soldiers.'

"He said: 'This is the Fort' (meaning his house) 'and I am the soldiers.'

At first I slept on the ground. Then one day an old sugar barrel floated up the river, and I hauled it ashore and used it to sleep in. Uncomfortable? Bless you, I just knocked out the head, and lay in it, and it was fine. Nice current of air all night. Most of the time I ate quail. Didn't have to shoot them. Just made a net and always had a supply. Well, things were going along fine, when I accidentally killed a pig, and had to skip down and live among the Seminole Indians for six months. (Better for me if I had shot a man.)

"During that time I discovered some of the phosphate beds that have made fortunes for others. Didn't know what phosphate was, and worse luck, didn't know that I could have squatted on 500 acres of land anywhere, and eventually owned it, it not having been surveyed by the U. S. Government at that time. Yes; I liked the Seminoles all right, only they

wouldn't talk, and I always liked folks to be sociable. But the alligators furnished plenty of music. We killed fully 1,000 during the time I was among the Indians, in 1876.

"When I came back to Sanford, I got another sugar barrel, and added it to my sleeping quarters. Then after some time, the captain of a steamer brought me down a piano box. Some time after this, I built a small room in the top of a live oak tree, and put a sign on it—'*No Boarders Wanted.*'

"Previous to that time there was no civilized person in the whole neighborhood but myself. Negroes were not allowed to stop there. Occasionally I saw some of the 'Cracker' people. The occasional visitor who got to coming to Sanford would take me for a wild man. And today, there is a town of 7,000 people where I lived in a sugar barrel, and the country thereabouts is well settled. When I first went there, some times as much as three weeks would pass without my seeing a soul.

"When the city was incorporated, in 1877, there were but 8 people living in Sanford who could vote, and its borders were extended to include the Swede settlement, three miles distant, so that there might be votes enough to make it a town. As I was inspector, and the Swedes could not read or write, I was their proxy, and did all the voting myself."

H. A. LUMSDEN

H. A. LUMSDEN

Born in Talbot County, Ga., Oct. 22, 1854, Mr. Lumsden emigrated to Orange County, Fla., in January, 1886, locating in Apopka. Later, he moved to Clay Spring, and afterward to Orlando, January, 1887.

He became a merchant and was so engaged for nine years, and was afterward appointed on the police force of the city, serving three years.

His business for many years has been connected with the city liveries, being a fine judge of horses and mules, and for several years past he has conducted a livery business in Orlando, and, although Orlando has the reputation of having more automobiles than any other Southern city (one to every fourteen inhabitants) the livery business is still of great importance as the demand for horses and mules seems never to diminish.

Mr. Lumsden is a hunter of reputation and his guidance has been sought by many sportsmen during the hunting season, for he knows the country and understands the game.

Many of the older citizens who were sportsmen first and business men on occasions, relish with satisfaction the memory of those fine old hunting days when they and "Lum" "took to the woods" and interviewed the quail and the turkey and frequently the deer and sometimes the bear.

A. A. STONE

A. A. STONE

A mile and a half northwest of Maitland lies the grove known for the past thirty years or more as the grove of A. A. Stone & Son.

This grove has been brought to its present state of productiveness ness through the ceaseless energy and sound business sense of A. A. Stone and his son, L. L. Stone.

The senior member of this partnership, Alvord Alonzo Stone, was born in Killingworth, Connecticut, August 24th, 1829. Though familiar with all kinds of farm work, he also learned the business of the fisherman, and from the age of sixteen to about forty he was captain of a crew that plied their craft successfully throughout the fishing season, April to November.

The winters furnished variety by affording the opportunity to get the ship timber which proved profitable employment.

He early showed great interest in grafting trees and many a tree of his neighbor's as well as his own orchard testifies still to his success in this line of work.

With such appreciation of tree culture it is not strange that Florida appealed to him as a most delightful place of residence. Accordingly, in 1883, the move was made from Guilford, Conn., his residence since 1867, to Maitland, Florida.

With the help of his son, L. L. Stone, he built a four-roomed dwelling, which became the ell of the house erected later.

In every community he and his good wife have always stood for the best things, while their married life, now rounding out sixty-five years, has been remarkable for its devotion and joy through all the changes that have come to them.

L. L. STONE

His orange grove was the first to come into bearing after the years spent in recruiting it from the destruction of the freeze and he helped to rehabilitate many another grove by setting his fine budded trees.

The junior member of this partnership, Lovell Lazell Stone, was born in Killingworth, Connecticut, November 16th, 1857.

In his tenth year the removal to Guilford took place, where his education was continued in the public schools of that thriving borough, including Guilford Institute, now the local high school. After a season's work with his father in the fishing business, he took a course at Eastman's Business College, Poughkeepsie, N. Y., which served him well in the business of these late years.

He became interested in Florida and came to the State in 1883 in company with his parents, and in the pioneer work that fell to their lot he made many friends who stood by him in many trying experiences, and in turn, he proved a firm friend to many in need.

He took special charge of the stone business which was carried on several years, and the good condition of that work today testifies to his thoroughness and reliability.

His daily life gave evidence of a strong Christian character. He was active in Sunday School work and in the cause of temperance.

On August 22nd, 1914, the bite of a rattlesnake caused his death, and his parents were deprived of the strong support that had borne them up so faithfully.

L. L. STONE

N. H. FOGG

N. H. FOGG

Boston has contributed a number of citizens to Orange County, but none more valuable than Mr. N. H. Fogg. In the earlier days, when the electrical profession was in its infancy, Mr. Fogg was an electrician in the employ of the R. H. White Dry Goods Co., of Boston. He came to Orange County, Florida, in 1884, locating in Altamonte Springs, where near this famous medicinal spring he has a fine grove and a beautiful home-place. He devoted his attention to the development of his own property, experimented in orange growing, pecan raising and in the cultivation of rare tropical and semi-tropical shrubs, trees, Japan cane, etc., giving the result of his experiments to the public far and near, through the various Florida newspapers of which he was the valued correspondent. His newspaper work was of an interesting order, always practical and yet very entertaining and whenever the name of N. H. Fogg was attached to an article in the Jacksonville Times-Union, Tampa Tribune, Orlando Reporter-Star, Sentinel and Citizen, one could always rest assured that there was something well worth reading at hand. In this way he has done some very excellent constructive work for Orange County, and many a man has received great encouragement from his many sketches.

For some years Mr. Fogg has been retired on his orange grove and takes life easy, resting assured that he has been among those valued early pioneers who have not lived in vain.

MRS. ELIZABETH M. SAUNDERS-MASSEY

Usually men are the earlier settlers in any new section, and it is so in Orange County; but there were some women who braved the hard life incident to the up-building of the county, and then there are others who arrived after the way had been blazed and homes and groves took the place of log cabins and forest.

Among these last named is Mrs. Saunders-Massey, who came to Orange County from Toronto, Canada, where her husband was connected with the Taylor Safe Manufacturing Company, turning out a product known the world over.

The primary object in coming to Florida was her son's health, and the sightly mansion on the hill-side and orange grove known as the "Hoosier Springs Grove" was selected with this in view. It is a most beautiful location, overlooking "The Three Graces" Lakes, "Faith," "Hope," and "Charity," which viewed when the setting Florida sun casts its many hued rays over the limpid waters, is a picture well worth an artist's vision.

Mrs. Saunders-Massy located in Orange County, but the dividing line of Seminole was ut immediately along her southward property line, so that she now lives in Seminole County. She can throw an orange across into Orange County.

ELIZABETH M. SAUNDERS-
MASSY

BERNHART HUPPLE

BERNHART HUPPLE

With his wife, Friederika, Mr. Hupple came from Gotha, Germany, in 1883, and located in Olivia, now Gotha, Orange County, Florida.

Originally a marble cutter, he found no opportunity in this line in his new home, and gave his attention to mill work and orange growing in the employ of Mr. Hemple, of Buffalo, N. Y., who developed a large property in Gotha.

Later he worked in fruit growing for Mr. Koehne. In the year 1885 he purchased the home place, including a farm of ten acres, which today is a model farm of its sort. In 1895 Mr. Hupple thought he would try the North, and worked for a time in Louisville, Ky., but the South appealed to him and Florida sand had gotten into his shoes and he soon came to the conclusion that, although there were draw-backs in Florida and Gotha was not altogether free from them, it was better here in the open, care-free life of a farmer, than in the over-populous hard-driven city, and he returned and went industriously to work, as a German always will, and determined to wrest success out of the ground. Here he lived, labored and finally died, aged 57, April 20, 1914.

His memory is cherished fondly by his family and friends, and his life and labors, although ended all too soon, will never be forgotten by them who loved him.

L. C. OSBORN

L. C. OSBORN AND WIFE

November 7th, 1881, this active citizen removed from Indiana to Zellwood, Florida, entering into the fruit business with his father, and later established a store in the town, doing business together from 1889 to 1913.

For twenty years he has held the responsible office of School Trustee and four years has been the postmaster. He is now also acting deputy of registration. He and family are members of the Methodist Episcopal Church, South.

Five children came to bless his household, one daughter and four sons.

W. T. BERRY

W. T. BERRY

In February of 1884, Mr. W. T. Berry left Russell County, Ala., for Orange County, Fla. After spending three years in fruit culture, in 1887 he entered into the mercantile line at Wekiva Springs for two years, and then turned his attention to railroading as agent for the Florida Midland, the T. O. & A., and in 1892 became connected with the Seaboard Air Line at Apopka, where he has served as station agent ever since, making twenty-four years of continuous railroad service, a fine record for a faithful man.

Mr. Berry not only proved himself a valued and faithful employee of the railroads, but he ranks as a good and useful citizen of his chosen town, where his attainments have been readily recognized and rewarded by the people.

No more honorable positions can be filled by any man than on the governing board of his city, where he is best known by friends and neighbors, and on the educational board, which has to do with the fitting of the on-coming generation. In these places Mr. Berry has evidenced his fitness by unremitting attention and fidelity. Apopka takes especial pride in her schools, for her citizens are among the first in the State, many of the first settlers having located there and many of them remained.

For fifteen years he served as town councilman, and for six years has been trustee of the public school district, for eight years alderman and for two years justice of the peace. All these offices he has filled with honor and fidelity. Mr. Berry was married in 1891, and has two children, Jeane V. and Thomas W.

TYRANNUS J. MINOR

Georgia has sent many good citizens down to Florida, and among them came Mr. T. J. Minor in December, 1885, locating at Crown Point. A farmer for years in Guyette County, Ga., he went into merchandising and upon coming to Florida he soon opened a store known as T. J. Minor & Brother, and except for four years, 1895-99, he has continued in business at Ocoee.

Ocoee was one of the earliest settled spots in Orange County and has ever been a busy place, surrounded with luxuriant orange groves and profitable gardens. The residents are community-loving folks and the prosperity of the section has depended on men of character and energy, and among these men Mr. Minor has been prominently identified as a community builder and as a business prospector.

In 1893 he was appointed postmaster and held the office 14 years, and was supervisor of the Ocoee schools for several years.

Twice he was a heavy loser by fire, in 1908,

and two years later, but with true Georgia grit he persevered and now owns 18 acres of orange groves, harvesting 1,000 boxes with prospects of increase this fall.

He, with J. O. Maguire, became interested in the Ocoee orange packing house and it is in successful operation to this day.

He became associated with the Citrus Exchange in 1909, and was its secretary till 1914.

Mr. Minor has a family of five daughters and one son.

TYRANNUS J. MINOR

JAMES W. GRAVES

J. W. GRAVES

J. W. Graves can safely be counted an original Orange County man, because he was born in Crown Point, Orange County, Fla., May 30, 1876.

After graduating in the county schools he engaged in farming and citrus fruit growing, in which he has been successful. He has been connected with the Ocoee orange packing house for twelve years and has demonstrated his ability in the business.

During the past season he has been extensively engaged in growing tomatoes and watermelons for market. His tomato farm covered ten acres and 250 acres of watermelons, truly a planter on a large scale. Mr. Graves and family, of wife and one child, Helen Louise, a little over two years of age, live in a pretty residence in Ocoee, though Mr. Graves is the owner of a fine ten-acre orange grove at Crown Point.

I. W. GRAVES

In the year 1871, Mr. Graves emigrated from Georgia, though the original family home was in North Carolina, where his father was a builder and contractor of considerable note. In those days the broad-ax was very useful in building, and he had a reputation for wielding this implement.

He was a true pioneer with all of the early settlers' instincts—and the new and wild sections of Florida held out many alluring inducements to him.

The question with him, as with many other newcomers seeking a home and fortune, was whether to locate along one of the natural water courses or go farther into the interior of the State, as each locality held out enticing inducements, somewhat differing in character and it was rather a difficult matter to decide which of the two would develop the sooner.

Mr. I. W. Graves first located at Titusville, on the Indian River, after a time moving to Lake Butler, Orange County, where he cleared the wild hammock and planted the Chase grove.

Here he lived for seven years and then removed to Crown Point, living there for seventeen years, all the while grew oranges and vegetables.

In 1903 he made a final move to Ocoee, where he has continued in his favorite line of business to this day. Men of this kind, the producers of the county, make her most valuable citizens. The children of this busy man and his wife are James W. Graves, Minnie M. Parramore,, Arthur F. Graves, Anna L. Rawlins, George T. Graves.

I. W. GRAVES

ELIJAH HAND

ELIJAH HAND

Mr. Elijah Hand recently died in Orlando, but while he lived he proved what one man could do in business life in Orange County. He came to Orlando from Shelbyville, Ind., in 1885.

His business was that of undertaker and furniture dealer. He was the leading undertaker in this section for many years, and established a business in furniture, carpets, etc., that compelled him to build larger quarters, resulting in the erection of the Hand building, which is located on the site of the old Magnolia hotel property on Pine street, the entire lower floors of which were devoted to his splendid business.

His foresight and keen business ability stood him in good stead at a time when many others could not see ahead very far, and by "taking time by the forelock" and building a spacious place where furniture, rugs, etc., could properly be exhibited, and then stocking with seasonable and elegant goods, he captured the public eye and demand at the same time and realized a speedy and substantial profit.

As a builder in the city, he left his mark for in addition to his own business block, he built a fine two-story brick on Orange avenue, and the handsome three-story brick, corner Orange avenue and Church street. Besides this, he was the owner of orange groves and timber lands and had a comfortable business property in Indiana.

Mr. Hand had two sons, Harry E. Hand and Carey Hand, the latter succeeding his father in the undertaking business.

MRS. MARY KERR DUKE

Mrs. Duke was the fourth child of John P. Kerr, Scottish born, and Sarah Howard Kerr, of North Carolina. She was born in North Carolina and soon after removed with her parents to Greensboro, Alabama, where she spent most of her girlhood. In 1857, the family removed to Dubuque, Iowa. While they lived in this northwestern city Mary was sent to the Elmira Female College, New York State, where by her ability, scholarship and delightful manners she distinguished herself, and after four years graduated with much distinction. While a student in this college, she had for a warm friend the Rev. Thomas K. Beecher, who had great admiration for her character and talents.

In about the year 1870 she was married to a Mississippi lawyer of high standing, Mr. Henry Gore Fernandez, who lived but a short time. Soon after his death, her daughter, Miss Hallie G. Fernandez, was born, and between whom and her mother subsisted until the hour of her mother's death, the most beautiful relations of mother, sister, sweetheart and friend.

Mrs. Duke came to Orange County about 1875, as a school teacher, being principal successively of schools at Fort Reed and Orlando. After Orlando was founded she made her home here and at length was married to Mr. James K. Duke, a Kentuckian. By him she had two sons, Robert Keith, dying in infancy and Buford Kerr Duke, a fine young man, honest, upright and intelligent and devoted to his mother.

Two years ago, Mrs. Duke's health began to fail, and in spite of the best medical attention in Orlando, she steadily lost ground. At length she went to John's Hopkins Hospital at Baltimore, where for eight weeks she was under the care of two distinguished physicians. She improved considerably and on their advice went to Atlantic City for a change of air, but as soon as she arrived there, she took a turn for the worse, and after one week passed away. Her end was painless and peaceful. "At eventide there shall be light" was fulfilled in her life's close.

Among Mrs. Duke's many ministries was her service to the Confederate soldiers confined in Northern prisons during the Civil war. Though living in the North, she was strongly Southern in her sympathies. She and her sister, Margaret, provided many comforts and luxuries for the Confederate prisoners, and the hearts of many poor lonely men were greatly strengthen. Some of the friendships formed during that awful period have survived to the present day.

On the organization of the South Florida Fair Association about twenty years ago, she was appointed Superintendent of the Department of Plants and Flowers, in which position her success was eminent and great crowds gathered daily to admire her handiwork.

During the World's Fair in Chicago, Mrs. Duke was appointed by the Governing Board of Lady Managers without her knowledge as one of the judges of horticultural exhibits. She accepted, being the only woman judge in that department, and gave the greatest satisfaction by her decision.

Above all, Mary Duke was a Christian, not of the protesting, talking type. She lived her religion and all who came in contact with her felt the reality of her faith. She has left the world better for having lived in it, and multitudes now that she is gone, rise up to call her blessed.

Entered into rest in Atlantic City, New Jersey, July 30th, 1913, after a long illness, one of the most gifted, brightest and kindest of women. She was a loyal friend, a faithful wife, and a loving mother. Interested in art, a student of general literature, and a fine writer, she was yet eminently practical in business affairs. One of her most pre-eminent traits was sympathy. If there were any cases of sickness, sorrow or poverty she was always one of the first to bring help. Her general optimism and charm of personality made her a host of friends. Interment was in the Kerr lot, Mt. Olivet cemetery, Nashville, Tenn., August 2nd, 1913.

Three Generations of Woodruffs in Orange County

ELIAS WOODRUFF

The original Orange County Woodruff was born in Elizabethtown, N. J. His father, Seth Woodruff was one of three brothers who came over to New Jersey from England.

Elias, of adventurous spirit, decided to look the country over a bit before locating for good, and amid his wanderings made his way to the newly constituted Mississippi territory, where, in Pike County, he settled upon a farm at China Grove. He married Miss Ailsey Collins, of Columbia, Marion County, and had eight children, six daughters and two sons, W. W. W. and Seth W.

Elias Woodruff was a soldier in Jackson's army, serving in the battle of Chalmette, New Orleans, La., 1815.

After many years spent in the quiet of home, the lure of adventure again possessed him, and his family now grown, he traveled to Mellonville, Orange County, Florida, arriving in 1844, and settled on Woodruff's Island at the head of Lake Monroe, the island and creek still bearing his name. Here for years he lived the life of a recluse in a log cabin of his own building, where he cultivated the island, which was remarkably fertile and produced vegetables of wondrous size and delicious flavor. Later he purchased land at Ft. Reed, where he planted an orange grove. In 1848, he sent to Mississippi for his youngest son, W. W., then seventeen years of age, who came to make his home with his father. They erected a cottage on the Ft. Reed grove, Elias going over to the island for days or weeks together. This house was the third frame house built in Orange County.

Mr. Woodruff was a great student and the last years of his life were spent quietly in his home with his son, and beloved books and papers.

He died in 1863, and was buried in the old cemetery, near Ft. Reed. Later the body was moved to Lakeview Cemetery, Sanford.

WILLIAM WASHINGTON WOODRUFF

W. W. WOODRUFF

The subject of this biography was born July 10th, 1831, in China Grove, Pike County, Miss. His parents were Elias and Ailsey Woodruff, pioneers of Mississippi. The father, having previously emigrated to Florida, sent for the son, who rode horseback from his Mississippi home to Mellonville, Orange County, after having tried the trip on a former occasion when sixteen years of age and found it at that time too difficult. In 1848 he built a home on an orange grove already established by his father.

Those were very exciting times on account of the

MRS. W. W. WOODRUFF

Seminole Indians, and William W. Woodruff entered the army and fought Indians from 1856 to 1857. In 1860 he married Miss Nannie Galloway, who had come to Florida with her father and lived at Rutland's Ferry. They began housekeeping on the Woodruff grove and kept open house, for Mr. Woodruff was of a generous and hospitable nature, and the visitor never felt himself a "stranger in a strange land" when in reach of the latch string of the Woodruff home and, in fact, there was seldom a time when there were no visitors there. Naturally a man of this nature early became interested in the public affairs of his county and State and in the convention known as the "Secession Convention," which met in Tallahassee in 1861, he was elected a delegate from Orange County, and was one of the seven men of that famous convention who voted against the ordinance of secession. Notwithstanding, while still in Tallahassee, he volunteered his services to the Southern army, but failing to pass the physical examination, he returned to his home in Orange County. As an indication of the method of traveling in those days it is interesting to note that he journeyed muleback to Gainesville, and there left the mule for the return trip, took the Yulee railroad to the Capitol.

Later in the strife Mr. Woodruff again offered his services to his State, and was accepted, joining the "Home Guards," Captain Watson, the officer in charge. This company had many thrilling experiences, at one time coming so near being captured that they had to abandon their horses while trying to make Cook's Ferry and swim the St. Johns River for safety.

After the war, Mr. Woodruff served his county two terms in the Florida Legislature. In 1869 the brothers and sisters of Mr. Woodruff insisted that he return to Mississippi and in response to their entreaties he sold all his possessions and returned there; but so strong a hold had Florida upon him that he came back within three months, located again at Ft. Reed, and started to make another orange grove. but never very strong, his health began to fail, and he only lived two years after returning.

The making of the new home depended largely upon his wife, when he died, February 14th, 1872. Being well educated and gifted with unusual personal ability, she gathered the remnants of property left and so planned, worked and lived to enjoy the income of one of the finest orange groves in Orange County.

Mr. and Mrs. Woodruff had three children: Seth, Emma and Frank. In 1877 Mrs. Woodruff married C. H. Beck and two sons were born. June 11th, 1909, Mrs. Nannie Woodruff Beck died in the home she had made, where her last days were spent in quiet and the enjoyment of her children, all of them residents of Sanford, except the eldest, Seth, who has for some years lived in Orlando, the county seat, where official duties demanded his presence.

SETH WOODRUFF

SETH WOODRUFF

Seth, the oldest of the third generation of Orange County Woodruffs, was born at Mellonville (Ft. Reed), March 10th, 1862. He attended the county schools, upon paying tuition, the schools of that time being free only to those unable to pay. He entered the Preparatory Department, Erskine College, Due West, South Carolina, in October, 1877, took the six years' course in five years, graduating in 1882 with A. B. degree and honorable mention in all branches of study. Upon returning home he entered upon a busy life of orange growing, trucking, cattle raising and mercantile business, which he followed for ten years, and during a part of the time engaged in public business, serving as clerk and assessor and tax collector and treasurer of Sanford, and as assistant tax assessor of the county.

In 1892 he was elected tax collector of Orange County and served in this capacity until 1904.

Upon terminating this public service he returned to his profitable business of cattle, trucking and orange growing. The writer could stop right here and enough would have been written to fill one man's busy life-time, but Mr. Woodruff has continued to crowd in many other things. A Democrat in politics, he has been actively connected practically all the while with precinct and county organization, and is now chairman of the Democratic Executive Committee of Orange County.

The public good has ever been in his thought and he has given unstintingly of his time and talents toward the promotion of many good causes. He was one of the small number who, in 1895, initiated the movement for hard-surfaced roads and now takes pride in the great system of county brick roads, which is the culmination of efforts along these lines.

He has encouraged the development of the public school interests into the splendid system now existing. He has always been deeply interested in legislative affairs and has actively promoted progressive laws for school, road, citrus, trucking and stock interests, and has contributed in service, time and money for every public and civic enterprise.

He was among the few who organized the Orlando Driving Park Association, out of which has developed the Orange County Fair Association, and the holding annually of a Sub-Tropical Mid-Winter Exposition, embracing four counties. He was president of the Fair Association during the first and second years and at the recent annual meeting in July, was again elected to that responsible position. He was president of the Orlando Board of Trade during 1911, and again in 1914, the rules of the board making the president ineligible for a successive term.

He served as city alderman for some years and as such was a careful and energetic city councilman.

He endorses all legitimate sports when conducted in a clean way and contributes to racing, baseball and polo, and is identified with social affairs and a stockholder in the Orlando Country Club. He is a hearty believer in fraternal organizations, and is a member of numerous fraternal orders.

Mr. Woodruff was happily married in 1896 to a native Florida lady, who was born and raised in Tallahassee, whose maiden name was Elizabeth Agnes Shine.

Mr. and Mrs. Woodruff enjoy a wide circle of friends and acquaintances, and with true Shine and Woodruff spirit, "the latch string" to their home always hangs on the outside. Seth enjoys and prizes the distinction of being a genuine "Florida Cracker," and while he does not recall having been consulted as to just where he should first see the light, he is perfectly satisfied that he should first have seen it among the orange groves, lakes and pines of old Orange County, Florida.

FRANK L. WOODRUFF

FRANK L. WOODRUFF   MRS. WOODRUFF   FRANK LEE, JR.   JOHN DEVLIN
RALPH GALLOWAY   HARRY SHINE

Mr. Frank L. Woodruff is the youngest son of Wm. W. Woodruff and Nannie J. Galloway. Was born at Fort Reed, near Sanford, Orange County, February 26th, 1871. Mr. Woodruff was educated in the Public Schools of Orange County, after which he spent two years in Erskine College, Dule West, S. C., where he met Miss Minnie Elizabeth Devlin, and they were married January 11th, 1897. Mr. Woodruff has been actively engaged in business in the county of his birth since 1892, and has held positions of trust and responsibility in the county of Orange and the city of Sanford, Fla. From 1896 to 1908 he was a member of the Democratic Executive Committee of Orange County. In 1910 he was elected County Commissioner for Orange County from the Sanford district. In 1912 he was re-elected, and in 1913, when Orange County was divided and Seminole created, he was appointed County Commissioner by Governor Park Trammell, and was elected chairman of the Board of County Commissioners in Seminole County. He has served on the Board of Aldermen of the city of Sanford three terms and was elected Mayor three times, 1903-1904-1906.

Mr. Woodruff is now engaged in business in Sanford, Seminole County, being the senior member of the firm of Woodruff & Watson, also being interested in the fire insurance and real estate business, also a director in the Seminole County Bank, and vice-president and director in the Peoples Bank of Sanford, Fla.

WILLIAM BENJ. HULL

WILLIAM BENJ. HULL

William Benjamin Hull and his wife, Emily Harriett Hull, arrived in Orange County, Dec. 25th, a glorious Christmas day, 1855. Coming from Cobb County, north of Atlanta, Ga., they first located at Ft. Reid and a year later moved to the neighborhood of Orlando and there made their home for the balance of their lives.

The original trip from Georgia was made by wagon and they were accompanied by a party of thirty-four persons, a part of whom were negro slaves, and this influx of new settlers, it is said, nearly doubled the population of Orange County.

In 1862 Mr. Hull joined Captain Joshua Mizell's company of "Home Guards," and went to Tallahassee, where the company was mustered into the regular army and they were quickly hurried to Virginia, where they soon saw service. Mr. Hull was twice wounded slightly by partially spent balls and later sustained a badly sprained ankle which sent him to the hospital. Reporting again for service he was captured at the first battle of Gettysburg and was taken to Ft. Delaware, where he spent twenty-three months, when the war closed and he came home.

Mr. Hull and wife were conducting a hotel in Orlando upon the outbreak of war and Mrs.

Hull continued the hotel during her husband's absence, and also acted as post mistress for the mail that arrived once each week. With the help of a faithful negro boy and girl, Mrs. Hull carried on a farm and probably the battle against starvation was never more energetically waged. Many times provisions ran very low, but soldiers' wives had a good friend in Capt. Mizell's father, who, too old to go to war, would, upon calling at the postoffice, make diligent inquiry as to the supply of food, and when Mrs. Hull was out of meat, "Uncle Dave" would butcher a beef and take a quarter to her.

The hotel had few guests during the war, but when court was in session, Mrs. Hull furnished dinner to every man in the county. The original dining table, somewhat reduced in size, is still doing service at the Hull home, southeast of the city.

Mr. Hull arrived home in July, 1865, having walked with a companion from Palatka, that being the terminus of the Federal boat line. Emaciated and foot-sore, he was in no condition to take up the battle of life, but this was no time for idleness, and as his companion during imprisonment was the fortunate owner of a blind horse, between them a cotton crop

THE HULL SISTERS

was grown of fifteen hundred pounds, and the price at that time being a dollar per pound, Mr. Hull's half interest brought $750, which enabled him to buy the property now occupied by Mr. W. L. Dolive as a home, besides other lands on which he moved. The following year he received $900 for his cotton crop, the price having dropped to fifty cents. This favorable price for long staple cotton soon enabled the thrifty soldier to rebuild his home, so long neglected.

Politically, Mr. Hull was a democrat, but was too modest and busy to take a very active part; with the exception of serving one term as county commissioner, although he did show considerable interest during the exciting days of "Carpet Bag Rule," in wresting the State from the hands of negroes and Carpet Baggers in 1876.

Mr. Hull was among the first to set out an orange grove and in 1875 proudly consigned his first crop of three barrels, from which he never received a report. In 1882 he sold his grove and moved across what is now the Conway brick road, where he spent the remainder of his life.

In early manhood Mr. Hull united with the Missionary Baptist Church, and his wife, who was a Presbyterian, joined with him, both becoming charter members of the First Baptist Church in Orlando. The recently completed Baptist Temple has a beautiful memorial window in memory of its last departed charter member, William B. Hull.

THE HULL BROTHERS

R. P. JEROME

HOME OF R. P. JEROME

The late R. P. Jerome came to Orange County, Fla., in 1886, arriving from the neighboring State of Georgia, where his earlier life was spent. He was an old Confederate soldier, having served from 1861 to 1865, with honor to his State. In the mercantile business at Blufton from 1865 to 1881, and upon moving to Florida he engaged in orange growing until the time of his death in 1913, at the good old age of 73.

Five children, three daughters and two sons, survived him. H. Jerome and his brother are engaged in the orange business.

R. EDGAR DANN

R. EDGAR DANN

For many years a stranger coming to Orlando would almost be sure to meet at the railroad station a jovial-faced man with glad hand extended, whose name was "Edgar Dann." For not only among the people of Orange County was this man well known, but far and wide he was remembered as the town booster and advertiser.

He was born in Ocoee, Orange County, and came to Orlando when fourteen years of age. His first occupation was night watchman for Mr. Monroe Mathews, retaining that position for ten years, then entering the transfer business on Church street, in which he became widely known, largely by reason of his annual booster publications which he sent broad-cast over the country. About two years prior to his death he became connected with the Dann Real Estate Agency, his brother being partner.

He was at one time assistant deputy sheriff under Sheriff Kirkwood.

One has written of him thus:

Big of body, big of heart, he was the friend of the old, the young, the great, the small. The writer knew "Big" Dann, as his friends affectionately called him, for a number of years, and enjoyed his friendship to the fullest. He was frequently thrown with him and he never saw a more even-tempered man, nor one whose heart was more easily moved. He gave of his means, but not of his anger, realizing no doubt that it is more blessed to give than to receive and that harsh words are not soon forgotten, but carry sorrow that lingers long.

Mr. Dann was the biggest "booster" Orlando had. He talked her advantages in season and out and showed the faith that was in him by putting every dollar he could into Orlando property. He proved his words by his deeds. He was the best posted man on the doings of the city that we can recall, and probably knew more people by their first name than any other man in Orange County. The tourist, the townsman, the "Cracker," were all alike to him. His big warm heart made him love them all and he showed his good feelings in a manner that no one could mistake.

Coming of parents who were not blessed with this world's goods, Mr. Dann not only brought himself up, but was a great help to the younger members of the family. He was one of those self-made men who did a good job of the making.

We regret that he is no longer among us and sorry that there are not more like him.

COL. JOHN NEILL BRADSHAW

COL. J. N. BRADSHAW

Among the citizens of Orange County from the years 1885 to 1904, the years of his connection with the Orange County courthouse, perhaps there was no man in the county better known than John N. Bradshaw.

Whole-souled and generous to a fault "Colonel Brad," as he was fondly called by the boys, was a friend in need and a friend indeed to all who applied.

This is no obituary, but a bouquet thrown at him while still living.

John N. Bradshaw was born October 20, 1862, in Covington, Georgia, and came to Orange County, Florida in the first full flush of virile manhood, on January first, 1883—just at the time when the eyes of the country were directed to the wonderful possibilities there were bound up in the orange industry. He first located in Apopka, Orange County, where his two older brothers, one of them now the Mayor of St. Petersburg, had settled in 1873.

It did not take so very long 'ere Mr. Bradshaw fitted into the active affairs of the county, for in November of the same year he removed to Orlando, where he occupied the position of deputy clerk of the Circuit Court of Orange County, under T. J. Shine, Circuit Court Clerk.

Occupying this place and coming into contact with the majority of the citizens of the county, among them many of the incoming settlers, he formed a large acquaintance, which in many instances ripened into friendships.

In July, 1887, he was appointed clerk of the Criminal Court, being the first clerk of the court.

At the Democratic primary, September 27th, 1890, he was nominated clerk of the Circuit Court, and took office in November, 1890, succeeding Shine.

He became a very popular officer and held this office for fourteen consecutive years, during which time he was conceded to be the best posted man in Orange County, politics —being acquainted with almost every foot of land and with the men living upon it.

In September, 1904, a complete reorganization in his affairs occurred, when after all these busy years in Orange County, he left the scene of his activities and many personal friendships and removed to Cameron, Texas, to settle a family estate of magnitude. Here he became president of the First National Bank of Cameron and continued as such for four years, when he sold his interests and removed to Amarillo, Texas, where he arrived in 1908 and engaged extensively in real estate.

Col. Bradshaw always said that when he got ready to really live he would certainly return to Orlando, and in December, 1911, his promise was fulfilled, for on that date he returned and found a partnership with Mr. Charles Lord in the real estate and fire insurance business, which he continues to this date.

Col. Bradshaw's military records is well known to the older citizens of Orange County, having served in the National Guard of Florida for nineteen continuous years.

He enlisted as a private in 1886, soon rose to lieutenant and then was elected captain of the crack company of the State. He went into the Spanish-American war as captain of company "C" 1st Regiment Florida Volunteer Infantry and left Orlando with 121 men and brought back every man alive at the close of the war.

The company was mustered out at Tallahassee, Florida, December 4th, 1898.

Captain Bradshaw's next promotion was that of Major 2nd Regiment Florida National Guard, and shortly thereafter Colonel of the same regiment.

On March 6th, 1905, after his removal to Texas, he was placed on the retired list with the rank of colonel. This in brief, completes his official and military record, but there is another side to the colonel's story, and that is his home life.

On Feb. 28th, 1905, he was married to Miss Elise Alexander, of St. Augustine, Fla., the loyal lady who followed his fortunes to Texas, and now happily lives with him on East Pine Street, Orlando, Florida.

JUDGE J. M. CHENEY

JUDGE J. M. CHENEY

Judge Cheney is in no sense a man whose usefulness has been confined to Orange County, Florida. His work has been State-wide and of such magnitude that only the fate of the political cards prevented a life tenure on the bench for the United States Southern District of Florida, where merit alone had placed him.

Born of an old line of Vermont parentage, January 6th, 1859, the boy, John Cheney, lived the life of the normal New England boy, a student in the common schools of Woodville, New Hampshire, and upon graduation entered the New Hampton Literary Institute, of New Hampton, N. H., where he graduated in 1881.

Selecting the law as his future profession, he entered the University Law School of Boston, Mass., where he secured the LL.B. degree in 1885.

And now he cast about for a suitable location and finally decided upon Orlando, Florida, where on December 29th, 1885, he duly arried.

In January, 1886, he associated himself with Author L. Odlin, under the firm name of Cheney & Odlin, attorneys, and almost instant success smiled upon him.

Besides his legal profession he early beaccame a developer of and booster for Orlando. Associated with others he installed the Orlando Water Company, at that time the finest outfit in the far South. Later there was added the Orlando Electric Lighting system, followed by the acquisition of the gas works, and the building of the largest ice plant in this section of the State.

These associated industries have been improved with every modern appliance and costly engines and dynamos, forming a most complete system.

Politically, Mr. Cheney is a Republican, and at once upon entering the State, took high council with the best and most honorable men of his party, having had much to do with its policies in the State.

He was elected City Attorney of Orlando, a non-partisan position, in 1889; was supervisor of the United States census for the State of Florda, under President McKinley in 1900. He was the nominee of his party for congress in 1900, and also in 1904, and a gubernatorial candidate in 1908.

In 1906 he was appointed by President Roosevelt, United States Attorney for the Southern District of Florida, and President Taft reappointed him in 1910.

In July, 1912, the president appointed him United States Judge from the Southern District of Florida, and took the oath of office on September 2nd. He presided with great satisfaction to the bar of the State until March 4, 1913, and right here is where the fate of party change stepped in, when the Democratic party succeeded and the Republican party in power and a majority of the Senate refused to confirm the appointments of retiring President Taft, although Judge Cheney's appointment had been made about eight months previously.

The judge accepted the decree with his customary optimistic good humor and has harbored no resentment, but re-opened his law practice in Orlando with his old-time success.

Judge Cheney was president of the Orlando Board of Trade for a number of years and it was under his administration and with his assistance that the first hard-surfaced roads in the county were built and a National Good Roads Convention held in Orlando. He has ever been a liberal and hard-working member of this body and the records show the result of his personality.

Fraternally, he is connected with the Orlando Lodge F. & A. M., being Worshipful Master in 1894; Royal Arch Chapter, of which he was High Priest in 1899, and a member of the Elks Lodge and is an active member of the Orlando Country Club.

MAHLON GORE

MAHLON GORE

Just at the opportune time when Orange County stood at the threshold of its first great stride forward, there appeared on the scene the man for the hour—a newspaper man, a man with a grasp of large ideals, a builder, not so much of houses as of ideas in the mass, an encourager and educator of men, a booster, a helper, an advisor.

This man was Mahlon Gore, who had been extensively identified with newspapers in the West for many years, and had charge of large development projects and who had practically retired from journalism because of failing health. To Florida he came, and to Orlando, where a great future unfolded itself before his mind's eye, and the enthusiasm of youth again took possession of him.

The Orange County Reporter was for sale at the time and Mr. Gore bought it and immediately converted it into the best news medium of this section, and the greatest booster in the State. Under his able experience and management the paper occupied a large place in the affairs of the county and became an information bureau and immigration agency combined, and was the direct means of bringing to Orange County and holding many valuable citizens.

Mr. Gore personally interested himself in the town and county and surrounding regions and vigorously fathered many an important enterprise. While a member of the town council, he framed and introduced the ordinance under which Orlando's famous oak shade trees were set out, and later served the city as Mayor for three successive terms and has always been a strong factor in the various Boards of Trade. Never a pessimist—always a booster to the extent of his means and ability, he has lived to the realization of many of his earlier dreams of Florida's development and is still at it.

EARL W. EWING

EARL W. EWING

This sterling young man was a native of Galia County, Ohio, where, after graduating from the public schools of his town, he came to Orange County, Florida, and settled in Winter Garden, where he immediately won many friends, and secured the esteem of the people of that section.

He identified himself with the live business interests of the community, engaging in the selling of real estate and as a merchant, which he prosecuted successfully.

Selling his mercantile business to the South Apopka Supply Company, he went more extensively into the real estate business and was building up a flattering trade in lands at the time his health gave way.

He was happily married to Miss Willie Carnell, and they were blest with a young son. Sad indeed was it that amid happy surroundings and a successful life and many friends, Mr. Ewing, at the early age of twenty-four, was called hence.

All who knew him contributed to the fact that he lived an upright, straight-forward life, quiet and kindly of spirit, courteous and considerate of others and that his death proved a sad loss not only to his immediate family and friends, but the town as well.

But even a few years of such a life proves of great value and as in his case left its imprint upon the times and the people. Mr. Ewing died February 2, 1913.

JOSEPH A. BARBER

JOS. A. BARBER AND WIFE

Joseph A. Barber was born at the south end of Lake Conway in Orange County, Florida, on December 18th, 1860.

Look backward a moment, some of us who claim to be old settlers and that date seems a long while ago.

He had only the advantages of a common school education, although that was considered of some importance at that early date in this section.

With this as his equipment and the natural gifts he was endowed with he has succeeded in the enterprises he has engaged in.

On March 10th, 1887, he married Miss Maggie S. Simmons, who was born Oct. 4th, 1869. She also is from a large family of the older settlers of Orange County.

Mr. and Mrs. Barber are the parents of a family of eleven children, all of them living at Conway and are occupied in farming, the most important of any occupation in the development of the country, as is evidenced by the "Back to the Soil" advocates of the present age, and the fact that nearly all the newcomers into Florida have that in view, whether fitted for it or not.

Added to farming this family are successful stock raisers and citrus growers, both profitable lines when properly handled, as most old-time Floridians know.

Mr. Barber remembers Orlando when its present corporate limits could not have contained over twenty inhabitants.

He remembers Orange County when its magnificent pine and oak forests were unbroken and when all kinds of game, both large and small, were abundant, and when its lakes and streams abounded in the finny tribe, when wolves, bears and panthers roamed the woods, when deer and turkeys ravaged the field crops, as do the rabbits today.

Mr. Barber did some of the work on the first railroad that ever crossed Orange County, viz: the South Florida Railroad, which was built in 1875. He well remembers the time when the town-site of Sanford was covered with virgin forest.

The home industries of this early time, 1862-1865, stand out vividly in his memory, when his mother took the cotton as it came from the field, ginned it, carded and spun it and wove it into cloth, afterward dyeing the cloth with any desirable color and making it into clothing for the family.

These are memories dear to the heart and there are others too sacred to mention.

For two years Mr. Barber was elected to and served as Tax Collector of Osceola County, 1890-94, and made final settlement with the county and State for the first seven years of that county's life.

He was not favorable to bonding Orange County, preferring that the county should remain as it was, without a dollar of debt against it, and he says he voted his convictions.

At the time of this writing Mr. Barber holds the honorable position as member of the County Democratic Executive Committee.

ANDREW J. BARBER

ANDREW J. BARBER AND WIFE

Andrew J. Barber is the son of William Barber and was born in North Florida, July 9, 1839.

His father died when Andrew was but two years of age. Sixteen years of his life was passed in Nassaua, Hernando and Columbia Counties.

He came to Orange County August 15th, 1855 and of course there was no Orlando, no Sanford, no Kissimmee. All was wild and the roads were but trails, many of them twining in and out through the woods, but all leading in the same general direction, and travel was by compass, the sun, and at night, by the stars.

The newest place of trade was Melonville on the south side of Lake Monroe—St. Johns River.

In those days Mr. Barber could count on his fingers the families residing in the county. It was the time of the Seminole Indian war, and Mr. Barber's chief business for twenty-one months was Indian fighting. He served during this time under Journegan, Bullock, Carter, Sparkman and Kendrick, and it was a life of excitement and adventure, as the history of the Seminole wars duly attest.

Those of us who are enjoying today the peace and prosperity brought about by the hardships of those early Indian fighters owe a debt of gratitude to such men as Mr. Barber, who bore the brunt of the battle, for no matter how much romance may be woven about the Indian and the disposition of his lands, the early fighter for the white race had in mind something much more practical to him and posterity, and that was the preservation of peace and the element of safety for his own home; hence he fought a desperate warfare from flowing stream to rising hillock, from behind the stately trees of the pine forests and amid the dense jungles of the black hammocks.

After the wars were over, the Indians dispersed and the remnant pressed down into the Everglades, Mr. Barber turned his attention to stock raising, for which parts of Orange County, as it then was, offered exceptional advantages, and as time went on he raised from the seed one of the finest orange groves in what became Osceola County, cut off from Orange.

Stock raising, orange growing and farming were his occupations through a long and useful life, and now in his 76th year of age, he lives over again in memory those earlier eventful and later peaceful scenes of the long ago.

HON. H. H. WITHERINGTON

H. H. WITHERINGTON

H. H. Witherington was born on a farm in Tuscaloosa County, Alabama, during the Civil war, in 1862. Came to Orange County, Fla., in 1883, and settled at Apopka, where he now lives. He was attracted to that section on account of its high rolling lands and ideal climate.

He began clerking in a grocery store, and later embarked in the mercantile business for himself, which he followed for twenty years continuously, during which time, assisted by Mayor John B. Steinmetz, of Clay Springs, he built and equipped probably the first rural telephone line in Orange County, and among the first in the State, in the year 1901.

Like most persons who came to Florida in those days, he began the task of making an orange grove, and to experiment in farming on a small scale. He soon was able to prove to the most skeptical that both corn and hay could be successfully grown on the high pine lands of Florida and has since been one of the few men who has grown his own stock feed from year to year.

Like many others, his hopes were somewhat blighted when the freeze of 1894 and 1895 killed his beautiful orange grove to the ground, and he wondered for a time whether or not the orange grove was worth the effort, but soon revived his courage and began rebuilding his once blighted prospects and is today rewarded by being the owner of a beautiful grove, which at harvest time each year shows forth its picture of green intermingled with yellow, and brings the usual dividend to the owner as a reward for his efforts.

He never aspired to political honors, although he was appointed in 1896 as member of the Board of Public Instruction of Orange County to fill the unexpired term of Hon. T. G. Hyers, and was re-elected and served continuously for fourteen years—declining to be elected again, claiming that there were younger and more capable men perhaps, who might fill the position more successfully.

The only distinctive honor claimed by him during these fourteen years of service was that the school interests were never once sacrificed for that of the individual.

He was married at the age of twenty-five to Anna Belle Turner, also of Alabama, an acquaintance of his boyhood days. To them were born five children—three boys and two girls, who are living and are practically grown.

Being a firm believer in the future possibilities of the State as a winter resort for older people from the Northern States, a healthful resort for the afflicted, a veritable pleasant resort for those able to afford it, a country, in fact, destined to become one of the most productive in fruits, vegetables and field crops of all kinds, with a climate unsurpassed, he decided to enter the real estate business and continually sings the praises of Florida, the State of his adoption.

HON. J. H. SADLER

J. H. SADLER

Orange County is cosmopolitan and the sons of many States contribute to her sturdy population. None more so than the scions of old South Carolina.

James H. Sadler was born in Anderson County, South Carolina, April 21, 1859, the son of James H. and Catherine E. Sadler.

The father laid down his life for his State in the Civil strife, in 1864, and the year following, the mother, with the three children, James H., Alice I., and Anna E., removed to her fathers, James G. Speer's home in Orange County, Florida, because her husband's estate was lost, being hastily closed up in fear of destruction at the hands of Sherman's army.

But very new and somewhat serious conditions awaited them in the newly adopted home. The nearest postoffice for all the region was Apopka, and the neighboring people took turn about in going for the mail once each week. Money—real money—was a very scarce article, and the interchange of help one to another had to take the place of laborers and money. Each helped the other do the thing most needed, and reserved a portion for still another helping at some future time.

Family life was rife in the district, for the whole neighborhood was as one great big whole-souled family.

A luxury-loving chap from the cities of indulgence might have voted the living of those days rather hard, consisting, as it did of cornbread, sweet potatoes, milk and hominy, beef, pork, fish and game of every sort, with biscuits

on Sunday—but it was no hardship for these royal folks who lived near to nature's heart and nature's God.

Sure, they made many sacrifices for each other, but then it all developed many big-hearted, unselfish, rugged characters, of which it is really refreshing to remember, in these days when modern advantages and conveniences enables one to live almost an isolated life so far as an out-stretched, helping human hand is concerned, the opportunity for mutual help being thus removed and the human appeal and helpfulness, one of the greatest pleasures of community life, and the best in human nature seems almost lost.

In these early times agriculture and horticulture were the only pursuits open to one and, naturally, these were entered into by Mr. Sadler as he grew to manhood's estate.

He married Miss Minnie M. Tilden, April 15th, 1887, and thus another link in the Speer-Sadler-Tilden chain was forged, and nine children have blessed this union, two sons are living in Colorado, one at Homestead, Dade County, Florida, and the others are home.

He believes in doing the best possible for his children and that the finest legacy he can leave them is to educate them, and this interest reaches out to the children of his townsmen, and the splendid school facilities he and his fellow citizens have helped to give to that section attest to the interest shown.

Mr. Sadler is reckoned a successful business man and has demonstrated this by giving his best thought and energy to the original lines he engaged in and by applying modern ideas and specializing. He was among the original growers of vegetables for Northern markets, and was also the first grower to irrigate his fields, which of itself opened up a new era in truck growing. Also, he has always been a successful orange grower and is possessed of real estate all over Orange County, in Dade County, and among the oil fields of Oklahoma. He was elected to the office of County Treasurer three successive terms and is now one of the Bond Trustees of the new brick road fund. He is president and director of the Bank of Oakland, director of the Winter Garden Water & Light Company and a director of the South Lake Apopka Citrus Growers' Association. This little sketch is simply set down for future reference, for the life of "Jim" Sadler is as an open book to all who know him and fortunate is he who calls him friend.

HON. SAMUEL S. GRIFFIN

HON. S. S. GRIFFIN

A Floridian in nativity and by inclination, Samuel S. Griffin was born in Gadsden County, Florida, November 5th, 1871.

He claims to be an early settler of Orange County by virtue of the fact that before he was one year of age his parents moved to Orange County, and naturally he accompanied them. He went to the public schools of the county and began early in years to take an active interest in the business of life.

His father was a mill man and the boy's first task was the humblest, but he steadily moved upward and when he became head-sawyer, he understood the timber and saw-milling business, because of having learned every detail.

His next adventure was railroading, and here again he started at the beginning and worked up to the top of the locomotive-engineering department, giving it up when he entered railroad contract work during the time of the Spanish-American war.

True to his instincts, he started modestly and so thoroughly worked up the business that he became the chief contractor in railroad ties on the lines of the Orlando Coast Line Railroad of the State.

So that, as may be seen, Mr. Griffin's chief characteristic is thoroughness, and this quality seems to govern him in his actions, private and public.

Thus, he saw the possibilities there were in the real estate business a few years ago and opened a small office and commenced to list a few properties and eventually he handled some of the finest land propositions in this section.

His political life records the same characteristics. He was for some years a member of the Orange County Democratic Executive Committee and in 1914 became a candidate for the State Legislature. Now, that he made good in the session of 1915, a number of his friends claim the honor of having "brought him out," but it is claimed by others that he is simply following the natural bent of his history and needed no one to "bring him out" or to "drive him," when once out. He originated several important legislative bills, one of them known as the Hotel Protection Bill, and was known among his colleagues as "The Investigator," that is, he never "went it blind," but believed in possessing the facts.

Mr. Griffin's family history records that he is the son of Lawrence Jefferson Griffin, whose native state was Georgia, and who was an honored Confederate soldier.

In 1901 Mr. Griffin married Miss Willie L. Vick, daughter of Ex-sheriff Vick, of Orange County, and they are the proud parents of three bright children, Misses Hilda, Helen and Master Stanley S. Griffin.

FREDERICK AUGUSTUS LEWTER

FREDERICK AUGUSTUS LEWTER

Mr. Lewter was born in Halifax county, N. C., on the 14th of December, 1854, and is a son of James Madison and Mary (Davis) Lewter, the former of whom traced his a n c e s t r y back to Martin Luther, the name having been c h a n g e d since the emigration of the American progenitor. The mother of the subject of this review was a second cousin of Jefferson Davis.

Frederick Augustus Lewter acquired his early education in Elm Grove and Buck Horn Academies in Hertford County, North Carolina, and spent his vacation (two summers) teaching school in Northampton County, North Carolina, and two years in the drug business with his uncle, Dr. John T. Lewter, in Murfreesboro, North Carolina, and later entered Richmond College, Richmond, Virginia. After leaving the latter institution he went to Philadelphia, arriving in the city in 1876, and there he spent one year as manager of several hotels. At the end of that time he returned to Halifax County, North Carolina, having succeeded to a large farm left by his father, and operated successfully three stores, until 1883, when his buildings were entirely destroyed by fire. After paying all his debts, Mr. Lewter found himself with a cash capital of sixty-eight dollars, and he determined to seek his fortune in other fields. Accordingly he moved to Florida, arriving in Orlando in 1884 with two dollars and thirty-five cents.

He secured a position in a general store in this city and after clerking for a short time, bought the enterprise, agreeing to pay for it within three years on monthly payments. So rapidly did he attain success, however, that the store was free from debt within one year thereafter. In 1885 he turned his attention to the real estate business, and he has since been continuously active along this line.

During the first ten years he sold land on a commission basis, but since that time has purchased his property outright and today owns valuable holdings in city and farming lands, and is perhaps the largest tax payer in this section of the state. His business has continualy increased for he has become known as an expert judge of land values and a man who never uses his knowledge or ability to defraud or inconvenience a client. By reason of his honorable and conscientious methods of dealing and his strict adherence to high standards of business integrity, Mr. Lewter has made an enviable reputation for himself and has built up a business which is one of the largest of its kind in this section of Florida. For a time he owned also the largest chicken farm in the State, having forty-four distinct breeds of chickens and as many as five thousand fowl. He sold twenty-thousand dollars' worth of eggs and chickens per annum and kept twenty-seven incubators in constant use. However, fire destroyed this enterprise some years ago, and he has since devoted all of his attention to his real-estate interests.

In 1885 Mr. Lewter was united in marriage to Miss Linnie Wilkins Holshouser, a daughter of William Simpson and Cynthia Ann Roberta (Dickenson) Holshouser, of Paris, Tennessee. Mr. and Mrs. Lewter have become the parents of the following children: Irma, Roberta, Laura Louise, Zelma Kight, Robert Dickenson, Medora Inez, William Frederick, Elva Jouett, Frederick Augustus, Jr., and Jewell. The family are devout members of the Presbyterian, Baptist and Methodist churches.

Mr. Lewter gives his allegiance to the democratic party, but is not an active politician, preferring to spend his leisure hours in his home, for he is a devoted husband and father. He is justly accorded a place among the prominent and representative citizens of Orlando, for he belongs to that class of men whose enterprising spirit is used not alone for their own benefit, but also for the advancement of community interests. He has excellent ability as an organizer, forms his plans readily and is determined in their execution. This has enabled him to encounter obstacles which would deter many a man and has been one of the salient features in his success.

WILLIAM SMITH

WILLIAM SMITH

Orlando and Orange County are indebted to men of every character for their cosmopolitan make-up. Some of these men assisted in the matter of the laws, the schools, the fraternal organizations, the churches and others left impress on the structural features of the city and its civic life.

Notably among these may be mentioned the late Hon. William Smith, who was a man possessed of many of the traits of his native land, added to those acquired by association and absorption in America.

He was born of Irish parentage, near Belfast, Ireland, April 13, 1855.

His mother died when he was an infant. His father came to America in 1859 and here the son, William, grew to manhood. He was educated in the public schools, and while still a young man, became superintendent of the Farrel Iron Foundry in Ansonia, Conn.

In the year 1885 he married Miss Elizabeth J. Miles, of Ansonia, and the following year they moved to Orlando, Florida, then just beginning to show evident signs of becoming a city.

With several associates he established The South Florida Foundry and Machine Company, and it was his close attention to business that had much to do with the quality of the structural iron that went into nearly all the business buildings in Orlando, which after all is a valuable monument to a man's usefulness in the community, for it will stand as long as one building remains in the city.

In the civic and governmental activities of the city, Mr. Smith had a large part. In the early days he became chief of the fire department, and thus he was not only a builder, but a preserver of Orlando.

For sixteen years he was a member of the city government, serving as councilman, on nearly every committee, and at the time of his death, less than two months had passed since the city government, of which he was president, had given place to the new order of commission government. Thus it may be said that with his demise, the old order passed away; and yet there will always be evidences of the new order in connection with his name, for, with the writer of this article, he was the prime mover for the first brick streets built in Orlando.

Religiously, Mr. Smith was a Presbyterian and held his membership in the First Presbyterian church of Orlando.

Fraternally he was conspicuous in the orders of Masons, Knights Templar, Knights of Pythias, Odd Fellows and Elks.

Mr. Smith passed away February 20, 1914, having written his name largely in the history of Orlando and his memory will ever be preserved in the hearts of those who knew him and who, with him, had some part in the upbuilding of Orlando.

Mr. Smith's family consists of his wife and two living daughters, one daughter and a son deceased. There are living three sisters and a half brother.

DAVID O. MAGUIRE

DAVID O. MAGUIRE

David O. Maguire was born in Gwinnett County, Ga., Oct. 16, 1850.

His father at that time was considered one of the substantial men of his county. At the close of the Civil war, fifteen years later, conditions were changed, slaves all free and almost everything gone but the land. Notwithstanding, he managed to attend Conyers Academy, Conyers, Ga., and after finishing there he taught school near his home for two or more years before he decided to attend the State University, Athens, Ga.

Temperate in his habits he made a good student. He studied political economy under Ben Hill, the noted Georgia Senator. He received a military training at the same university.

Upon finishing his education at this place he accepted the position of principal of the High School of Loganville, Ga., where he taught for several years.

He was married to Miss Margaret M. Francis, also a college honor graduate, Jan. 7, 1880.

His health failing, he decided to come to Florida and engage in orange culture. This occupation at that time was very alluring and promised a fortune in the near future.

James Maguire, an older brother, came with him. They toured the State in a light two-horse buggy, finally deciding to buy land near Lake Apopka, now known as Crown Point, to which place he brought his family two years later.

He bought the Pennington Grove in 1890, where he moved the same year. The freeze of 1894-5 killed his groves to the ground, but he sanguinly went to work to bring them back to bearing.

He was instrumental in bringing about the Citrus Exchange, together with T. J. Minor, built and equipped the Exchange packing house at Ocoee, and was president of the Exchange at that place. He never tired of doing what he could to help the community in which he lived. As a man he was honest and reliable and thoroughly unselfish. He was a close student of politics and helped organize the People's Party and attended the convention when the platform was adopted.

He gave his five children, four sons and one daughter, the advantage of a college education. The oldest, Dr. Thomas C. Maguire, now has a good practice at Plant City; Charles Hugh Maguire graduated from the State University at the same time as his brother and went to Washington and Lee to study law, but died suddenly of appendicitis on February 6, 1911; Fred H. Maguire, at Ocoee, and Rayner F. Maguire, attorney at law, Orlando, Fla.; Lillian Irmer, a student at Tallahassee, Fla.

At the age of 63, November 9, 1913, Mr. Maguire went to sleep on the night of the eighth, never to awaken. His death was a shock to his family because so unexpected.

JOSEPH M. LEWIS

J. M. LEWIS

Boston contributed to Orange County when Mr. Lewis arrived at Altamonte in 1881. Here he was employed by Crisey & Norris, builders, and later he built the Altamonte Springs Hotel, the Frost House and directly or indirectly built nearly every house in the place. His principal business now is superintending orange groves in addition to having six large groves of his own, Altamonte and vicinity producing some of the finest fruit in the counties of Orange and Seminole.

Mr. Lewis tried out California in '49, and the fact that he located in Florida and has, as a self-made man, wrested success out of the primeval forests and helped to convert this beautiful spot at Altamonte Springs into one of the rarest places in the State proves the value of Florida in comparison with California. Mr. Lewis has two sons, Arthur A. and James M., and one daughter, Miss Grace.

CAPT. J. C. STEWART

CAPT. J. C. STEWART AND WIFE

Capt. J. C. Stewart came to Orange County in 1854 and settled at Clay Spring, now known as Wekiwa Springs. After spending one year there among the wild beasts, such as wolves, bears, panthers and wild-cats, he moved about three miles west, where he took up a homestead, built up a home and resided till he was called to fight for his country. He was exempt from going to war on account of holding the offices of tax assessor, collector, census taker and sheriff, but at the solicitation of his many friends to go as their captain, he sacrificed everything—home, wife and a family of eight bright children. The struggle must have been a hard one.

He was a high Mason and known among friends as a "peace-maker" in times of unsettled differences among neighbors. He was also a sincere Christian, a member of the Baptist denomination. He was always foremost in all things educational and for the upbuilding and betterment of his country.

Owing to severe climate hardships and many privations, he died the first year of the war leaving a heart-broken wife with the care and bringing up of eight children, which she did in a most highly respectable manner. Nothing in a complimentary way along these lines could be overdrawn, for she was a strong woman mentally, physically and spiritually. She must have been to bring up that many children alone in the pioneer days, when there were no public schools in the country. She was able to give all the children a common school education.

JAMES L. GILES

JAMES L. GILES

Mr. Giles anti-dates most of us who came to Orange County, for he has been here since his birth.

With a public school education he entered actively into business life and the success which has followed his endeavors by some people is called "good fortune" or "luck," but is simply the applied force of the man who knows how.

He is first of all a keen business man, with extraordinary fore-seeing and far-seeing ability, with methods at once direct and courageous. His is no faint-hearted theory, but even while the iron is heating, he strikes.

First and last Mr. Giles is a builder. This does not mean that he has confined his efforts to buildings, for he is the owner of thousands of acres of unimproved lands on the St. Johns River, in Seminole County and Orange County, besides profitable orange groves and farms.

But he is the man responsible for many of the finest structures in Orlando, among them what was originally known as the Charleston—now the Watkins Block, the Orlando Bank and Trust Company building, the Orlando Telephone Company building, the Astor Hotel building, "Dixie," that elegant residence property on North Lake Lucerne, three other fine residences on the same lake, a number of modern homes throughout the city and recently the finest colonial residence in this section of the State, costing about $30,000, which is to be his permanent home.

It is in large tracts of land and in improved property that Mr. Giles especially interests himself as a real estate dealer. Many of the finest sales in the county having been made through his agency or directly of his own holdings.

Mr. Giles has always been closely identified with the commercial life of the city through the Board of Trade and otherwise. One of the earlier organizers of the Board of Trade, he has given of time and means without stint for the up-building and advancement of the city's best interests.

One of the originators of the Orlando Driving Park Association, he became one of the charter incorporators of the Fair Association, and has been treasurer and director of the same since its inception.

He was also one of the organizers and the president of the Orlando Country Club, controlling the finest golf course in Florida.

Personally and socially Mr. Giles is free-hearted and free-handed, an interesting acquaintance and a friend, generous and loyal.

His family consists of wife, son, Leroy B. Gies, attorney-at-law, daughter, Mrs. Allen Weathersbee, and younger daughter, Miss Edna Adelima.

HON. MOSES O. OVERSTREET

HON. M. O. OVERSTREET

The self-made man sometimes generates into a selfish man, but not so in the case of M. O. Overstreet. He has a keen realization of what "self-made" means to any aspiring individual who has no "pull" other than his own strong will, and therefore, although exceptionally successful beyond the attainments of many others, he is approachable and charitably hearted to others who are attempting to climb.

A Georgian by birth, his first round on the ladder was the naval stores business, which he modestly entered and aquired a personal knowledge of in every detail.

After a time he removed to Orange County, Florida, where he continued in the same line for a while, acquiring large tracts of timber land, both for the turpentine and lumber, and in 1906 bought a half interest in the Warnell Lumber Company Mills, later forming the corporation of the Overstreet Crate Company, with a capital of $200,000 and turning out orange boxes and crate material in very large quantities, 1,250,000 orange boxes and vegetable crates in like proportion annually, employing 325 hands and sustaining a whole town at Lockhart. Besides, he is the owner of four turpentine stills, the Overstreet Turpentine Company, being capitalized at $200,000. The company has about thirteen miles of private railroad as feeders to the mills and stills.

Thus, he is one of the largest manufacturers in the State of Florida and the largest in this section of the state.

Commercially he is president of the Peoples National Bank of Orlando, an institution which has become very popular, a stockholder and director of The Heard National Bank of Jacksonville, and of hotel properties in Jacksonville and Atlanta, Ga.

He has been a progressive in public affairs, holding important offices for years in the Orlando Board of Trade and in the Fair Association and is always among foremost citizens in the promotion of every good cause.

Politically he has held notable city and county offices, having been on the Orlando city council, as alderman, for years, and very active in city affairs; is now chairman of the Orange County Commissioners, a position he has held for several successive terms, and was one of the foremost advocates of permanent brick roads, which are being built all over the county under his administration.

So pre-eminently successful has his official career been that he is now being favorably spoken of as the next State Senator of his district. Although very busy in every possible line, Mr. Overstreet put one even over himself during the present year, when the Baptist church organization needed a man with extraordinary executive ability to enable them to build a church worth $35,000. Mr. Overstreet undertook the matter and within a few months completed the finest Baptist church in South Florida.

Mr. Overstreet is a family man, and particularly lives in the enjoyment of home life. He was married to Miss R. Ethelyn Chapman, daughter of Mr. and Mrs. John T. Chapman, of Plymouth, Florida, April 12th, 1900, and they have four children: Robert T., Hazel, Elizabeth and Mildred, and the family residence is located in one of the finest and most spacious park-like locations in the city of Orlando.

HON. J. L. DILLARD

HON. J. L. DILLARD

Mr. Dillard may safely be called half Virginian and half Floridian, for he lived one-half· of his lifetime in each of these wonderful states.

A native of Staunton, Va., he arrived in Winter Garden Florida, in the year 1888 when the interest was at its height for that time. Adopting fruit culture and gardening, he originally rented lands and cultivated on shares with Sheriff J. H. Vick on the property then known as the "Washington Place," the beautiful little town of Winter Garden now being located on a part of that property.

He spent six continuous years in this line of business, and about 1895, when the crop industry was entirely destroyed he concluded he had an even chance with the other growers, and planted largely in orange and grapefruit trees. Foreseeing the inevitable growth of Winter Garden because of its splendid location and climate and the possibilities of its exceptionally fine lands, he invested in town property, which continued to grow in value, by day and night, and finally the light broke upon a very prosperous and constantly increasing little city, and Mr. Dillard's dream came true.

Mr. Dillard was too busy a man to care for public office, but it came to him, as it will sometimes to the man who is successful in his own affairs. He was elected a councilman by his townspeople and later he was elected County Commissioner of Orange County, holding the office at this time.

He applies the same practical tactics to public business which he has given to his private concerns and was an advocate for the new brick county roads, now building. Mr. Dillard may safely be said to be a constructive citizen of Orange County.

MRS. HELEN ROLLINS

MRS. HELEN ROLLINS

The lady whose picture appears on this page was born in Salem, Mich., September 24, 1833, her maiden name being Helen Augusta Jackson, daughter of Joseph Jackson. She was married to Mr. John H. Rollins July 3, 1854, at Crown Point, Ind.

They came from Burlington, Ind., to Florida, in 1884, on a trip for investigation, and in May, 1885, bought property in Winter Park, induced thereto by the fact that Mr. Rollins was related to Mr. A. W. Rollins, for whom Rollins College was named.

In 1886 they removed permanently to Orlando, where Mr. Rollins engaged in fruit culture and also sold his invention, a patent plant cover.

Mr. Rollins died in 1903, and his wife, being a very energetic woman, gifted with a knowledge of values and possibilities of the future invested in real estate with considerable profit.

Until within a very short time before her death, on April 15, 1915, she showed no evidence of infirmity, having had the above protograph taken only a few weeks prior. Her age was eighty-one years and her Christian faith was that of the Congregational Church.

She had two children, Flora Estelle, who died in infancy, and Stella Alcesta, now Mrs. S. H. Happersett, who lives on Lake Eola, Orlando, Florida.

FIRST PUBLIC SCHOOL HOUSE IN ORLANDO

OLD-TIME ROAD THROUGH ORANGE COUNTY PINES

Index

Compiler's Notes:

This book is reproduced from the original volume printed in 1915. Photographs in the original volume were much better than in this reprint — even with scanning and enhancing, photographs do not photocopy well. A few photographs were poor in the original. There are copies of the original publication in the Orlando Public Library's Local History section as well as in the Orange County Regional History Center's Library and Archives (both in Orlando).

While this book is entitled "Early Settlers of Orange County, Florida", there are many names conspicuous by their absence. One would certainly expect to see the names of Jernigan, Hull and Patrick — some of the earliest settlers in the area. Names like Bumby, Hyer, Howe, Hughey, Ivey, Parramore, Shine, Summerlin and many others should be among the influential early settlers of the region.

Preliminary research has provided no definitive answer as to why these particular pioneers were selected, but some possibilities emerge. In W. R. O'Neal's *Memoirs of a Pioneer* column in the Orlando newspaper in 1944, he wrote that Clarence E. Howard, pioneer photographer of Orlando, produced a card with 51 negatives of men who had sittings with him. He called this "Some of the Men Who Made Orlando". It may be that these photos were the basis of this book. Another possibility is that these were members of the Orange County Pioneers' Association, which was in existence from 1911 to 1928.

We hope to publish a future volume or two, which will include more of the pioneer families of Orange County. If you are descended from an early settler and have information or photos that could be used in a future volume, please contact the compiler at the CFGS address below.

Central Florida Genealogical Society, Inc.
P. O. Box 536309,
Orlando, FL 32853-6309
www.geocities.com/cfgscfgs

2001